T0297963

America Celebrates

FLORENCE GRAY-SUTTLE

Copyright © 2011 by Florence Gray-Suttle. 87425-GRAY
Library of Congress Control Number: 2011901372
ISBN: Softcover   978-1-4568-5983-1
         Hardcover   978-1-4568-5984-8

All rights reserved. No part of this book may be reproduced
or transmitted in any form or by any means, electronic or
mechanical, including photocopying, recording, or by any
information storage and retrieval system, without permission
in writing from the copyright owner.

This book was printed in the United States of America.

To order additional copies of this book, contact:
Xlibris Corporation
1-888-795-4274
www.Xlibris.com
Orders@Xlibris.com

CONTENTS

NEW YEAR'S DAY MENU #1

Appetizer

Salmon Mousse
Chilled Champagne/Sparkling Wine

Main Course

Black Angus Standing Rib Roast Beef with Horseradish Sauce
Sautéed Red Cabbage with Pepper Sauce
Black-eyed Pea Patties
Country Bread with Savory Seasonings Butter
Hearty Red Wine

Dessert

Apple Dumplings with Cinnamon Ice Cream
Fresh Brewed Coffee

Salmon Mousse

1 16 ounce can Salmon

1 8 ounce package Cream Cheese

1 10 ½ ounce can Cream of Mushroom Soup

½ cup chopped Green Onions

1 Cucumber, thinly sliced

8 envelopes unflavored Gelatin

¼ cup boiling water

¼ cup fresh Dill

½ cup chopped Celery

Warm the soup and cream cheese in a large saucepan; blend until smooth. Dissolve the gelatin in hot water, add to the cheese and soup mixture and stir. Add the rest of the ingredients (except Cucumber Slices) and mix until blended. Pour into five-cup mold. Chill until firm. (Flavors enhance when chilled for 24 hours). Unmold when ready to serve and top with cucumber slices if desired. Serve with assorted crackers. Suitable for freezing.

Yield 20 servings.

MARKETLIST: 16 oz can Salmon, 8 oz package Cream Cheese, 10 oz can Cream of Mushroom Soup, Green Onions, Celery, Unflavored Gelatin, fresh Dill, Cucumbers, Standing Rib Roast of Beef (Black Angus), prepared Horseradish Sauce, Red Cabbage, Black eyed Peas Uresh}, whole cloves Garlic, Crushed Red Pepper Flakes, Apple Cider Vinegar, sliced Bacon, fresh Jalapeno Peppers, fresh Cilantro, Walnuts, Dark Raisins, baking Apples, Maple Syrup, prepared Pie Crusts (if desired) Vanilla Ice Cream, coffee beans for grinding, a Sparkling Wine or Champagne, red wine (recommend a Cabernet Sauvignon), Lemons, Limes, variety crackers.

Black Angus Standing Rib Roast Beef With Horseradish Sauce

Select one four pound (Four Rib Roast) for four guests. Prepare a second four rib roast for additional guests (avoid preparing larger than four ribs per roast for accurate cooking times and ease of carving and serving). Season the roast with Course Ground Black Pepper and lightly sprinkle with Sea Salt. Place fat side up uncovered in pan measuring at least 10" X 12" X 2". Roast in 325 Degree Oven for 2-½ –3 hours until a meat thermometer temperature of 140 Degrees (rare) or longer in order to reach a 160 Degree (medium) temperature. It is not recommended that this meat is cooked to a well-done (170 Degree – plus) temperature. Check meat thermometer often to avoid over-cooking this roast. Baste Roast often with pan drippings.

To carve this roast, slice meat from bottom of roast to create flat surface—place roast on a warmed serving platter. Insert a long pronged fork below the first rib and slice top rib. Remove carving knife and slice along the rib bone with the tip of the carving knife. Lift the slice with the carving knife to side of platter. Drizzle pan juices over slices and serve with Horseradish Sauce—continue until roast is carved.

Horseradish Sauce

1-½ cup Heavy Cream

2 Tablespoons grated Horseradish

Tablespoon of grated Lemon Rind

Juice of a large Lemon

Teaspoon of Paprika

One large Clove of Garlic – grated fine

One half teaspoon of Sea Salt

Beat cream to thick consistency, add all ingredients and mix well. Taste and adjust seasonings as desired. Return to refrigerator or place briefly in the freezer. Serve very cold.

N O T E : A Sour Cream Horseradish Sauce is easily prepared by mixing grated Horseradish and Sour Cream to taste and adding granulated garlic and lemon juice. There are also a number of very flavorful Horseradish items on grocery shelves including those "ground", "creamed" and others stored in vinegar and/or herbs.

Sautéed Red Cabbage

1 large head Red Cabbage

Cored and coarsely sliced

2 Tablespoons Canola Oil

3-4 cloves chopped Garlic

1 Tablespoon Crushed Red Pepper

Salt to taste

Coarse Ground Pepper to taste

One bunch chopped Green Onions

¾ Cup Apple Cider Vinegar

¼ lb. crisp Bacon, crumbled

Heat Canola Oil and Olive Oil in skillet until hot. Heap Cabbage, Garlic, Pepper and Salt in skilleSauté. Add Onions and Garlic and sauté. Drain off the oil, add Crushed Red Pepper and Cider Vinegar. Cook till Cabbage is just tender. Sprinkle crumbled Bacon on Cabbage and serve immediately.

Black-Eyed Pea Patties

1 package fresh Black-Eyed Peas

2 Tablespoons Flou

2 Eggs, beaten

1 small White Onion, chopped

6-8 Green Onions, chopped

½ pound Bacon

2 fresh Jalapeno Peppers,
cored, seeded and chopped

½ cup Cilantro, chopped

1 Tablespoon Black Pepper, Salt to taste

Fry or microwave Bacon until crisp. Cool and crush.

Rinse fresh Black-eyed Peas in colander, then cook until soft. Drain, reserving ½ cup of liquid.

Mix reserved liquid with Flour, add Eggs, and mix well. Add remaining ingredients. Form mixture into patties and pan fry in small amount of vegetable oil until brown and cooked through.

Country Bread With Sweet And Savory Seasonings Butter

1 package dry Yeast

1 ¼ cup warm water

2 cups Bread Flour

5 cups Bread Flour

1 cup Wheat Flour

1-½ cup warm water

1 teaspoon Salt

Dissolve Yeast in ¼ cup warm water and let stand until foamy. Add to mixture 1 cup warm water and beat in 2 cups of Bread Flour. Cover mixture and allow to stand for 10 – 12 hours.

Combine Wheat Flour, water, salt and 3-4 cups Bread Flour. Mix all ingredients and knead flour into dough to form a firm smooth surface loaf and add flour as needed. Place dough in warm area and allow to rise until 2-½ – 3 times in size. Punch down and allow to rise a second time until doubled in size. Prepare oven to steam using a small baking dish filled with boiling water in oven for 5 minutes. Remove and bake bread for 35 – 40 minutes until crust is golden brown and bread sounds hollow when tapped.

Flavored/Seasoned Butters

Herb Butter

1 stick (8 Tablespoons) sweet, unsalted Butter

1 Tablespoon finely chopped herb of your choice

Cream Butter and Herb. Shape, cover and refrigerate several hours before use.

FLAVORED/SEASONED BUTTERS (CONTINUED)

Honey Butter

2 sticks unsalted sweet cream Butter

1 Tablespoon Honey

1 Tablespoon Powdered Sugar

Soften Butter (do not melt). Chill Honey approximately one hour. Combine ingredients and cream together. Shape into 1 inch balls and drop into ice water to solidify or shape as desired. Place on server and refrigerate. Serve with country bread, waffles, toast or muffins. Wrap in saran wrap before refrigerating. Keeps well for several days refrigerated.

Strawberry Butter

1 8 ounce package Cream Cheese

1 stick sweet cream unsalted Butter

¾ cup Powdered Sugar

12 large ripe Strawberries

1 teaspoon Vanilla

Cream Butter, Cream Cheese and Powdered Sugar and mix well. Chop berries (not too fine) and stir in (leaving small pieces of berries) and add Vanilla. Shape as desired and refrigerate before serving.

Lemon Butter

1 stick (8 Tablespoons) sweet, unsalted Butter

Juice of 2 Lemons

2-3 Tablespoons freshly chopped Parsley

Melt Butter. Add Lemon Juice and chopped Parsley. Flavor vegetables and seafood dishes with this Butter.

Maitre de'Hotel Butter

1 stick (8 Tablespoons) sweet, unsalted Butter

Salt, pepper and cayenne to taste

2 Tablespoons minced Parsley

1 Tablespoon Lemon Juice

Cream softened Butter. Add chopped Parsley, Salt, Pepper and Cayenne. Work in 1 Tablespoon Lemon Juice. When thoroughly blended, shape, chill and serve cold. Wonderful with broiled seafood/fish dishes, steaks and chops.

Italian Herb-Garlic Butter

½ cup Butter, softened

1 Tablespoon chopped fresh Parsley

1 Tablespoon Lemon Juice

½ teaspoon Italian Herb Seasoning

2 Cloves of Garlic, chopped fine

Combine all ingredients, stir well. Serve with steak, corn on the cob, or Country Bread. Refrigerate up to one week, or freeze up to three months.

Apple Dumplings

3 Tablespoons Butter, softened

1 Tablespoon Dark Raisins

¾ teaspoon Cinnamon

½ cup Maple-blended Syrup

3 Tablespoons Sugar

1 Tablespoons chopped Walnuts

4 medium Baking Apples (about 2 lbs.)

Purchase prepared rolled pie crusts, your favorite packaged pie crust mix or see pie crust recipe, below. Form pastry into ball, wrap in waxed paper and refrigerate until well chilled. In small bowl, combine Butter, Sugar, Raisins, Chopped Walnuts and Cinnamon. Mix well. Pare and core Apples. Fill center of each with Raisin/Walnut mixture. Preheat oven to 375 degrees F. Generously grease 13"X9"X2" baking dish. Divide pastry into fourths. On lightly floured surface, roll out each part from center to edge to make 7" squares. Trim edges, using pastry wheel, if desired. Reserve trimmings. Place an Apple in center of each square. Bring each corner of square to top of apple, pinch edges of pastry together firmly to cover Apple completely. Re-roll pastry trimmings. With leaf-shaped cookie cutter, cut as many leaves as possible. Brush leaves with cold water and pres on top of dumplings. Arrange dumplings in prepared baking dish. Brush top and sides of each with some of the maple-blended syrup. Bake, brushing occasionally with syrup, 40 minutes until pastry is a rich golden brown and apples seem tender when tested with wooden pick. With broad spatula, remove to serving dish. Serve with Cinnamon Ice Cream. Yield 4 servings.

Cinnamon Ice Cream

1 cup Whipping Cream

¼ cup superfine Sugar

1 teaspoon Cinnamon

One half gallon ice cream

½ cup Pecan bits

Whip the Cream with Sugar. Fold in Cinnamon. Soften ice cream and swirl in whipped cream mixture. Refreeze. Serve with warm Apple Dumplings and sprinkle top with Pecan bits.

Pie Crust

2-½ cups Flour

1 teaspoon Salt

1 cup Vegetable Shortening

6 Tablespoons Cold Water (more if needed)

Combine Flour and Salt, Cut in Shortening with pastry blender until mixture resembles course meal. Sprinkle water on top and stir until dough holds together when pressed. Slowly add small amounts of water and stir until dough holds together. Shape the dough into four round discs. Wrap and refrigerate until well chilled. Flour flat surface and roll each disc thin and follow directions for Apple Dumpling recipe.

NEW YEAR'S DAY MENU #2

Appetizer

Individual Bowls of Black Eyed Pea Soup Seasoned with Smoked Ham and topped with Chopped Green Onions
Serve with Jalapeno Corn Bread Sticks
Bloody Bulls

Main Course

Charcoal Grilled Main Lobster Tails served with Melted Lemon Butter
Black Angus Beef Filet Mignon in Pepper Marinade
Potato, Onion and Cheddar Cheese Casserole
Loaves of Home Made French Bread
Pinot Noir

Dessert

German Style (Old Style) Peach Cobbler (not Pie)
Fresh Ground/Brewed Coffee

Black Eyed Pea Soup Seasoned with Smoked Ham and Topped with Cilantro and Chopped Green Onions

3-½ cups fresh Black-eyed Peas

3 cups Chicken Stock or canned low-fat Broth

Half pound cooked Smoked Ham, chopped

1 small white onion, chopped

2 Tablespoons Balsamic Vinegar or

Red Wine Vinegar

3 large Garlic Cloves, minced

1 Bay Leaf

½ teaspoon dried Thyme, crumbled

¼ teaspoon dried crushed Red Pepper

4 – 6 chopped green onions for topping

Cilantro, washed and divided into small sprigs

Crisp Bacon Strips, Crushed

Cook Smoked Ham Hocks in boiling water until tender and outside smoked skin and bone can be easily removed. Chop into 1" pieces. Bring remaining ingredients to a slow simmer in a heavy, large pot (reserving Green Onions and Cilantro sprigs for garnish) and cook until peas are tender, stirring occasionally, about 45 minutes. Remove Bay Leaf, season to taste with Salt and Pepper, serve in individual soup bowls and top with sprinkling of chopped green onions and sprigs of Cilantro. For additional flavor and texture fry lean bacon until crisp and add crumbled bacon pieces to the soup just before serving.

MARKET LIST: Fresh Black Eyed Peas, Smoked Ham Hocks, Green and White Onions, Bacon, Cilantro, Bay Leaf, Lobster Tails, Black Angus Filets, Irish Potatoes, Fresh Herbs, Canned Peaches, Bloody Mary Mix Items (see recipe), Pinot Noir, Grated Cheddar Cheese, Grated Velveeta Cheese, Half and Half Milk/Cream, Corn Meal, Butter, Jalapenos, Balsamic or Red Wine Vinegar, Cilantro, dried Thyme, Crushed Red Pepper, Pablano Pepper, Red and Green Bell Peppers, Worcestershire Sauce, Flour and Corn Meal, Coffee, Charcoal and flavored smoking woods, Teriyaki sauce, Italian Dressing, whole Garlic Cloves, Olive Oil and Salad Oil, Sea Salt and course ground Black Pepper.

Jalapeno Corn Bread Sticks

2 cups Yellow Corn Meal

2/3 cups Flour

4 teaspoons Baking Powder

1 teaspoon Salt

½ cup canned chopped mild Jalapenos Peppers (drained)

½ cup canned chopped Pimento Peppers (drained)

1 1/3 cup Milk

2 Eggs, beaten

¼ cup Vegetable Oil

2 teaspoons Sugar (optional

Preheat oven to 450 degrees F. Oil the corn bread stick or other heavy cast iron molds. Combine Corn Meal and dry ingredients, add Milk and Egg and stir. Add Vegetable Oil and mix thoroughly. Add chopped and drained jalapeno Peppers and Pimento and stir well. Oil and pre-heat corn bread stick pans or other mold and fill with mixture. Bake in hot oven (450 degrees) for 15 – 20 minutes. Turn onto warm bread tray and serve with Butter.

Bloody Bulls

1 48 ounce can low-salt Tomato Juice

3 10 ½ ounce cans of Campbell's Beef Broth

10 ounces Lemon Juice (fill one broth can)

20 dashes Tabasco Pepper Sauce (to taste)

10-15 dashes Tabasco Jalapeno Sauce (to taste)

¼ cup Worcestershire Sauce

20 dashes Celery Salt

20 dashes Black Pepper

7 dashes Dill Weed

10 dashes each: Celery Powder, Sea Salt, Lemon Pepper, Onion Powder

Thoroughly mix all ingredients and store in large glass jar (capped) in refrigerator. Keeps for several weeks. To Serve: Pour mix over ice in glass and add Vodka as desired. Stir and garnish with Celery, Dilled Green Beans, Olives or Pickled Okra.

Charcoal Grilled Maine Lobster Tails

Use fresh Maine Lobster if available – if not, thaw and wash frozen lobster tails in cold water. Clip the inside covering over the tail – leaving the hard back and tail in place.

Prepare a marinade of: 2 cloves chopped Garlic; 1 cup Teriyaki Sauce; 1 medium bottle Italian Dressing. Place Lobster Tails shell side down and pour the marinade over the tails. Refrigerate up to two hours.

Remove from marinade, lift the tail from inside the shell, leaving the shell attached and place on a hot charcoal or mesquite grill. Rotate the tails frequently and when cooked, serve on a large heated platter (gently replacing the tail meat into the hard shell).

Melt two sticks of Butter, squeeze the juice of one lemon into the Butter and serve with the Lobster Tails. Add sections of lemons and limes on the serving platter.

Beef Filet Mignon Pepper Marinade

2 cloves Garlic

½ red Bell Pepper

½ green Bell Pepper

6-8 small bunches Parsley

Sprinkle of Crushed Red Pepper

¾ cup Olive Oil

½ cup chopped Green Onion

1 Poblano Pepper, roasted, seeded, peeled and chopped

1 Jalapeno Pepper, roasted peeled, seeded and chopped

2 Tablespoons Worcestershire Sauce

1 Tablespoon Course Ground Black Pepper

This marinade is adequate for four 2-inch thick Beef Filet Mignons. Chop 2 cloves of Garlic, Red Bell Pepper and 6 – 8 small bunches of Parsley. Roast, peel and chop Green Bell Pepper and Yellow Bell Pepper and mix with Garlic, Pepper and Parsley. Add ½ cup of chopped Green Onion tips and 1 chopped roasted Pablano Pepper with 1 chopped Roasted Jalapeno (if using) to the mix. Add 1 Tablespoon of course ground Black Pepper and a few sprinkles of Crushed Red Pepper. Add ¾ cup Olive Oil and 2 Tablespoons of Worcestershire Sauce. Place steaks in marinade in refrigerator for a minimum of 2 hours or overnight.

Place Filets on hot Charcoal Grill (add moistened chips of Hickory or other fragrant woods) and cook until desired doneness. It is not recommended to cook the Filet Mignon past the "medium" done stage. Pour marinade over steaks while cooking.

Serve on platter with Grilled Lobster Tails.

Potato, White Onion and Cheddar Cheese Casserole

5 medium/large peeled and sliced Potatoes

One and half cup Whole Milk

One stick of Butter – sliced

4-6 ounces of chopped or grated Velveeta Cheese

Salt and Course Ground Black Pepper to taste

1 large White Onion, peeled and sliced

½ cup Half and Half

1 8 ounce package Grated Cheddar Cheese

Mix all ingredients in large mixing bowl and place in 8 inch round or 8x8 inch baking dish or casserole.

Bake in 375 degree oven until brown and cooked through.

French Bread

2 (¼ ounce) envelopes rapid-rise Yeast	1 Tablespoon Butter, softened
2 Tablespoons Sugar	6 ½ - 7 cups Flour, divided
2 ½ cups warm Water (105-115 degrees)	1 Egg White
1 Tablespoon Salt	1 Tablespoon Cold Water

Combine first 3 ingredients in a 1-quart liquid measuring cup; let stand 5 minutes. Stir together Yeast mixture, salt and Butter in a large mixing bowl. Gradually stir in enough Flour to make a soft dough. Place in a well-greased bowl, turn to grease top. Cover and let rise in a warm place (85 degrees) free from drafts, 40 minutes or until double in bulk.

Punch dough down; turn out onto a lightly floured surface and knead lightly 4 or 5 times. Divide dough in half. Roll one portion into a 15 X 10 inch rectangle. Roll up dough, starting at long side, pressing firmly to eliminate air pockets; pinch ends to seal and turn under. Press seam side down on a greased baking sheet sprinkled with cornmeal. Repeat procedure with remaining dough.

Cover and let rise in a warm place, free from drafts, 30 minutes or until doubled in bulk. Make 4 or 5 (¼ inch deep) cuts on top of each loaf with a sharp knife. Bake at 400 degrees for 25 minutes. Combine egg white and water; brush over loaves. Bake 5 more minutes. Yield 2 Loaves.

Peach Cobbler-German Style

Filling	Batter
5 cups sliced peeled Peaches (about 3 lbs)	½ cup unsifted Flour
¼ cup Water	½ cup Sugar
½ cup Sugar	½ teaspoon Baking Powder
2 Tablespoons Flour	¼ teaspoon Salt
1 Tablespoon Lemon Juice	2 Tablespoons Butter
½ teaspoon Vanilla	1 Egg slightly beaten
½ teaspoon Almond Extract	¼ teaspoon each Cinnamon and Salt
2 Tablespoons of Butter	

Preheat oven to 375 degrees.

Make filling. In medium bowl combine Peaches, Sugar, Flour, Lemon Juice, Vanilla and Almond extracts, Cinnamon, Salt and ¼ cup Water. Turn into 8X8X2 inch baking dish. Dot with 2 Tablespoons Butter.

Make Batter. In medium bowl, combine all batter ingredients, beat with wooden spoon until smooth. Drop in 9 portions over filling, spacing evenly. Batter will spread during baking. Bake 35 to 40 minutes, or until peaches are tender and crust is golden. Serve warm with Vanilla Ice Cream.

Chinese New Year

There are so many historical and unique ways to celebrate the Chinese New Year. And while this book attempts to present some of the special flavors and foods sometimes included in the celebrations, it will offer only a glimpse into the unique and wonderful world of Chinese Foods. The preparation techniques combined with a varied and brilliant use of raw meats, fish, vegetables and seasonings has created the most popular food choice in the world today.

Chinese Teas are popular around the world and are produced in over twenty Chinese provinces. Types of teas include the Green Tea, very popular in the United States and believed to have anti-aging, anti-cancer and anti-bacterial properties. Red Tea, Black Tea, both have high concentration of Caffeine and are the most popular teas in Europe and South Asia. The more highly fermented teas include Pu-erh Tea and Oolong Tea. Flowers, herbs and roots are used to flavor teas and among the flowers used are Jasmine, Gardenia, magnolia and the rose.

The New Year is the most popular and celebrated holiday in the Chinese culture and preparations for the celebrations can begin months before the event and continue for 15 days. The eve of the Chinese New Year is the most exciting event and traditions and rituals are very carefully observed. The ancient custom of Hong Bao, meaning Red Packet (envelope) is practiced on the first day of the new year and includes presenting money in red envelopes to children and unmarried adults by married couples. The tradition of visiting and greeting family and friends and forgiving and forgetting grudges and past grievances is practiced on the first new years' day also.

The Chinese Calendar and Zodiac, the twelve animals that govern specific years, are widely featured in Chinese restaurants in the United States. The ancient calendar dates from 2600BC when Emperor Huang Ti introduced the first cycle of the Chinese Zodiac. On the western calendar, the start of the new year falls on Sunday, February 3, 2011 and is the year of the Rabbit. The Chinese New Year begins on January 23, 2012, is the year of the Dragon, Feb 10 for 2013 is the year of the Snake, January 31, 2014 is the year of the Horse and February 19, 2015 is the year of the Sheep. The other animal signs are Monkey, Rooster, Dog, Pig, Rat, Ox and Tiger. The sign under which you are born is said to have strong influences in your life.

If you have not used the Chinese wok, Rice cooker or Bamboo Steamer, I hope that this section of the book will encourage you to become acquainted with these cooking techniques. Stir frying is a very practical, time saving and easy method of preparing delicious dishes and an opportunity to design your own combination of meats, vegetables, seasonings and sauces for the flavors you most enjoy.

CHINESE NEW YEAR MENU #1

Appetizer

Hoisin-Glazed Pork Ribs
Fat and Juicy Egg Rolls
Fried Won Tons
Fruit Punch

Main Course

Steamed Sea Bass cooked with Scallions and Ginger
Chinese Long Rice
Zucchini with Mushrooms Chinese Style
Jai

Chinese Sticky Cake (Nian Gao)
Hot Tea

Hoisin-Glazed Pork Ribs

1 cup Catsup

¾ cup Hoisin Sauce*

½ cup Honey

5 Tablespoons Soy Sauce

5 Tablespoons Dry Sherry

¼ cup plus 2 teaspoons White Wine Vinegar

¼ cup Sesame Seeds

2 Tablespoons plus 2 teaspoons Curry Powder

2 Tablespoons plus 2 teaspoons Oriental Sesame Oil

2 Tablespoons grated Orange Peel

1 Tablespoons salted Black Beans, minced*

2 Tablespoons minced Garlic

1 Tablespoon Chili Paste with Garlic*

3 pounds Pork Baby Back Ribs

Whisk all ingredients except ribs in large bowl to blend. Divide Ribs between 2 large baking dishes. Brush with half of sauce. Cover Ribs and remaining Sauce (separately) and refrigerate overnight.

Preheat oven to 375 Degrees. Transfer Ribs to heavy large baking sheets. Roast ribs until tender, basting frequently with some of the remaining Sauce, about 1 hour.

Place remaining sauce in heavy small sauce pan and bring to simmer. Transfer Ribs to platter. Cut into individual Ribs and serve, passing remaining sauce separately.

*Available at Asian markets and some supermarkets.

Fat and Juicy Shrimp Egg Rolls

1 pound Pork, chopped fine

8-10 ounces raw Shrimp (peeled, deveined and tailless)

1 Tablespoon Cooking Oil

2 cups finely chopped Cabbage

½ cup finely chopped Mushroom

¼ cup shredded Carrot

¼ cup Soy Sauce

1 teaspoon Cornstarch

½ cup chopped Celery

½ cup chopped Green Onions

12 to 14 Chinese Egg Roll Wrappers

Oil for deep frying

Chinese Mustard

Ginger Soy Sauce

In Wok or skillet, stir-fry Pork in 1 Tablespoon oil till brown, remove from pan. Add vegetables to pan and cook covered 2-3 minutes, adding small amount of oil if needed. Blend Soy Sauce and Cornstarch and add to vegetable mixture along with Shrimp and Pork. Cook and stir till thickened and bubbly. Remove from heat. Generously fill and roll 12 to 14 Egg Roll Wrappers, setting filled rolls aside and covering with towel.

Prepare deep fryer with vegetable oil sufficient to deep fry Egg Rolls. Fry until golden brown - 3 to 5 minutes. Drain on paper towel. Keep warm. Serve hot with Chinese Mustard and Ginger Soy. Makes 12 to 14 Egg Rolls.

MARKET LIST: Specialty/Asian Market Items: Hoisin Sauce, Chili Paste, Black Beans, minced. Supermarket items: Wonton Wrappers, Curry Powder, Oriental Sesame Oil, Oranges, Garlic, Soy Sauce, Honey, dry Sherry, Sesame Seeds, Catsup, Chinese Style Long Rice, Zucchini Squash, Mushrooms, Green Onions, Pork Ribs, whole Sea Bass, Shrimp, Pork, Cabbage, Eggs, Fruit Punch and Fruit to dress, Vegetable Oil, Chinese Tea/Green Tea, Brown Sugar, Rice Flour, Dates, (preserved Plums, Candied Orange Peel may be used), Milk, Fresh Gingerroot, Chicken, Carrots, Oyster Sauce (if desired).

Wontons

1 Garlic Clove Sliced

½ teaspoon sliced fresh Gingerroot

1 cup diced cooked Chicken

1 cup chopped fresh Mushrooms

1 Green Onion, sliced

1 Tablespoon Soy Sauce

1 teaspoon Oyster Sauce if desired

32 to 36 Wonton Skins

1 Egg beaten

egetable Oil for frying

¼ cup sliced Carrot

1 teaspoon Cornstarch

2 teaspoons dry Sherry or Rice Wine Vinegar

Process Garlic and Gingerroot in food processor fitted with metal blade, until minced. Add remaining ingredients except Wonton Skins, Egg and Oil. Process until mixture is finely chopped.

Place one Wonton skin on working surface with one corner facing you. Cover remaining skins with damp paper towel. Spoon one rounded teaspoon of filling just below center of Wonton Skin. Fold the corner closest to you toward the center and over filling, leaving one inch of top corner unrolled. With finger, moisten right corner with egg. Bring left corner to center, fold right corner over left corner pressing together firmly to seal. Set aside – repeat for remaining wontons.

In deep fryer, heat 2-3 inches of oil to 350 degrees. Fry wontons a few at a time for 3 to 4 minutes until golden brown (turning once). Drain on paper towels. Serve warm with a variety of dipping sauces, I.e., sweet and sour, plum sauce or hot mustard.

Steamed Sea Bass with Scallions and Ginger

1 and ½ pound Sea Bass (may use Flounder), cleaned, scaled and the spongy matter inside the head (gills) removed

Dry Sherry or Shao Hsing Wine*

Fresh Gingerroot

Scallions, chopped

Rinse the fish inside and out with small quantity of wine. Select a round or oval platter large enough to hold the fish and will fit inside the top of a steaming pan/vessel. If you do not have a clam steamer or Chinese bamboo steamer, use a large metal pan half full of water and bring to a boil. Place the fish on the platter, sprinkle Sherry Wine and spread fresh Ginger and Scallions over the fish and set the platter on a rack over the boiling water, cover and steam for 10 – 15 minutes (or longer depending upon the size of the fish). When cooked, remove the platter and pour off the liquid that has accumulated around fish. Sprinkle Scallions over fish and serve.

Chinese Long Rice

2 cups raw extra-long-grain rice

3 cups water

Pour the Rice into a colander/sieve and rinse it thoroughly under cold running water until the water runs clear. Drain. Add the Rice to a saucepan and add the water. For softer rice, add a small (½ cup) of water. Cook the Rice, uncovered over high heat about 10 minutes, or until "fish eyes" (tiny craters) form over the surface of the Rice. Cover with a tight fitting lid and cook over very low heat about 15 - 20 minutes longer. Rice should be fluffy and separate easily.

Zucchini With Mushrooms Chinese Style

2 pounds small Zucchini

½ pound fresh Mushrooms

¼ cup oil

¼ teaspoon Salt

1 Tablespoon Soy Sauce

½ cup chicken Broth

2 teaspoons Cornstarch mixed with

3 Tablespoons cold water

Wash and trim the stems of Zucchini and slice diagonally in ¼ " slices. Rinse and trim Mushroom stems and slice vertically. Saute Mushrooms in oil briefly and add Squash, stir-fry until Zucchini is well coated with oil. Add remaining ingredients except Cornstarch mixture and bring to a boil. Cover and simmer until Zucchini is tender and bright green. Thicken with Cornstarch mixture and serve immediately.

Chinese Sticky Cake (Nian Gao)

¾ cup Water

½ cup Brown Sugar

1 ¼ cups glutinous Rice Flour

1 Egg

2 Tablespoons Milk

½ cup chopped Dates (preserved Plums or Candied Orange Peel can be used)

Boil water. Mix Brown Sugar and water to make a paste, cool. Add Flour, Egg and Milk and stir to blend. Knead the dough until smooth, then add chopped sweets. Pour batter into lightly greased 7" shallow cake pan. Place a pan half full of Hot Water on lower rack in oven at 400 degrees one half hour before preparing cake. Place cake on middle rack and steam for 35-45 minutes (until edges release from the sides of the pan). Allow to cool and unmold. Slice thin to serve.

CHINESE NEW YEAR MENU #2

Appetizer

Jien Duy (Sweet Sesame Seed Ball)
Crab Rangoon

Soup

Egg Drop Soup

Main Course

General Chicken
Mandarin Fried Rice

Sweetened Fruit Drink
Variety of Teas

Jien Duy

Jien Duy are deep fried, puffed, glutinous rice balls filled with red or black bean or lotus paste and covered with sesame seeds. The small rounds of dough transform into large airy puffs when fried. The belief is that successful businesses are created similarly – the entrepreneur can turn a small amount of capital into a big return.

1 1/3 cup Water
4-5 sticks Chinese brown slab Sugar
1 pound glutinous Rice Powder/Flour
1 cup canned Sweet Red Bean Paste filling
(or Black Bean or Lotus Paste)
½ cup Sesame Seeds
Peanut Oil for deep frying

Boil water and Sugar till Sugar is dissolved. In a large bowl put Rice Powder and pour Sugar water over – stir thoroughly until a smooth dough forms. Knead. Roll dough into two 1-½ inch logs. Cut into 1 ½ inch rounds. Roll into a ball. Flatten ball and place a ½ inch piece of bean paste in the center. Fold dough over and roll into a smooth ball to enclose the filling. With wet hands dip ball into sesame seeds to coat. Press the seeds to adhere. Repeat with remaining dough. Heat oil to 325 degrees and carefully drop balls into hot oil and fry for 12 to 15 minutes.

Crab Rangoon

½ pound fresh Crabmeat (drained and chopped)

    Or canned Crabmeat (drained)

½ teaspoon of Zesty Sauce or Steak Sauce

½ teaspoon fresh Garlic, chopped fine

8 oz package Cream Cheese

36 Wonton wrappers

2 Egg Yolks, beaten

Combine Crabmeat, Steak Sauce, Garlic and Cream Cheese, stir well. Place mixture in center of each Wonton wrapper and bring four corners together, press and seal closed. Brush each with Egg Yolk and drop into Vegetable Oil at 375 degrees until golden brown.

Egg Drop Soup

Two cans Chicken Broth

1 Tablespoon Cornstarch

1 Egg, well beaten

2 Tablespoons sliced green onion

In saucepan place the Tablespoon Cornstarch and whisk or stir in the Chicken Broth. Cook until slightly thickened. Add the egg streaming slowly and stirring gently. Remove from heat, add the Green Onion and serve.

Mandarin Fried Rice

Canola Oil

2 Tablespoons minced Garlic

3 Eggs

2 Tablespoons minced Ginger

1 bunch chopped Scallions, green and white separated

1 Lapchang, diced (Chinese Sausage), (Substitute 4 strips cooked Bacon if desired)

3 cups cooked, day old long grain rice

3 Tablespoons thin Soy Sauce

½ teaspoon White Pepper

Salt to taste

Prepare wok—place 2 Tablespoons of oil and quickly soft scramble Eggs. Remove the eggs. Using same wok, coat with oil and stir fry Garlic and Ginger. Add white Scalloins and Lapchang. Add Rice and toss to mix thoroughly during stir fry. Add Soy Sauce, White Pepper and Scrambled Eggs. Taste and adjust seasonings.

General Chicken

1 Lb. boneless, skinless Chicken, cut in large chunks

1/3 cup Cornstarch

1 small Zucchini, cut into chunks

2 teaspoons minced Garlic

1 Tablespoon chopped Green Onion

¼ cup Chicken Broth

1 tsp Oyster Sauce

¼ tsp hot Pepper Paste

1 Tablespoon Soy Sauce

1 Tablespoon Rice Wine

3 Tablespoons Rice Vinegar

1 ½ Tablespoons Cornstarch mixed with 1 ½ tablespoon Water

1 teaspoon Sesame Oil

Cut the Chicken into large pieces and coat with Cornstarch. Set aside. Slice Zucchini on a diagonal – 1 inch wide. Roll the Zucchini and reverse the slice to form trapezoid shape. Combine Garlic and Green Onion in a small dish. Combine Broth, Oyster Sauce, Soy Sauce, Hot Pepper Sauce, Wine and Vinegar in a small bowl. In another dish or small glass, mix Cornstarch with Water. Place a metal strainer in a large receptacle (not plastic) in the kitchen sink.

Heat wok over high heat for two or three minutes. Add Vegetable Oil and heat to very hot. Add Chicken, stir. Fry until golden brown. Transfer Chicken to strainer.

Place empty wok back on high heat for 30 seconds. Add garlic mixture and fry for several seconds. Add Zucchini and toss a minute over high heat. Add sauce mixture and bring to a boil. Add Cornstarch and boil until thickened. Add Chicken and Sesame Oil and heat through.

MARKET LIST: Sesame Seeds, Peanut Oil, Vegetable Oil, Glutinous Rice Flour, Sweet Red Bean Paste (or Black Bean), Brown Sugar, Zucchini Squash, Mushrooms, Soy Sauce, Chicken Broth, Cornstarch, Eggs, Dates or Candied Orange Peel, Long Grain Rice, Chicken, Green Onions, Milk, Crabmeat, Cream Cheese, Wonton Wrappers, Cream Cheese, Lapchang, Garlic, Ginger, Oyster Sauce, Rice Wine and Rice Vinegar, Sesame Oil, Variety of Chinese Teas.

Valentine's Day Dinner for Two Menu #1

Appetizer

Artichokes with Herbed Mayonnaise Dip
Chilled Champagne

Salad

Stuffed Tomato with Herbed Croutons

Main Course

Filet Mignon En Croute
Grilled Mixed Vegetables with baby Red New Potatoes
Mini French Loaves w/Herbed Butter
Merlot

Dessert

Individual Heart Shaped Hershey's Chocolate Cake with Cherry Topping
Cappuccino Amaretto

Artichokes with Herbed Mayonnaise Dip

Trim the sharp pointed tips from cleaned Artichokes. Place in a deep pan with about 2 inches of salted water, 2 Tablespoons of Lemon Juice and a clove of Garlic. Bring to a boil, immediately turn heat to low and simmer, covered until leaves are easy to remove.

Serve with seasoned mayonnaise.

Mix sea salt and course ground black pepper to taste in one cup of mayonnaise. Add ½ teaspoon each of chopped Garlic, thyme, lemon juice and 1 teaspoon chopped parsley to mayonnaise and stir well. Artichokes leaves are best served warm and when leaves are gone, cut heart into serving pieces. Dip leaves of heart of chokes into seasoned mayonnaise and enjoy.

MARKET LIST: For the Sweetheart menu, you will need large, ripe Tomatoes, White and Green Onions, black Olives (seeded), fresh Asparagus, packaged croutons or bread and Butter for home made croutons, Artichokes, two 6 or 8 Ounce Beef Filets, boxed Pie Crusts or your pie crust recipe ingredients, mushrooms, commercial Mayonnaise, fresh Garlic, fresh Lemons, Blue Cheese Crumbles and Blue Cheese and Blue Cheese Dressing, Leaf Lettuce, Bacon, Celery, Red and Green Bell Peppers, Yellow Squash, Zucchini Squash, Teriyaki Sauce, Italian Dressing, Eggs, Milk, Sugar, Hershey's Cocoa, Butter, Vanilla, Milk, Powdered Sugar, Baking Soda, Cherry Pie Filling and fresh Strawberries if desired.

Stuffed Tomato with Herbed Croutons

Lettuce, Green Leafy

One Medium/Large Cored Tomato

Green Onions

Black Olives (Seeded)

Steamed and chilled fresh Asparagus

Croutons (See Instructions below)

Slice the tips of the Green Onions lengthwise and soak in ice water until they curl. Place a Lettuce Leaf on a chilled salad plate. Shred approximately one cup of leaf lettuce and place on top of the whole leaf. Cut the stem and top off the Tomato and remove a small amount of the core. Place on the bed of Lettuce. Fill the Tomato with the Blue Cheese Dressing, then place the Onions into the dressing in the Tomato, leaving the curls outside. Arrange the olives on the Salad. Snip off the ends of the Asparagus and add to the Salad. Then garnish with crushed crisp Bacon. Serve with your choice of salad crackers or homemade Croutons – see below.

Dressing

Blue Cheese Crumbles

Any Commercial Blue Cheese Dressing

Mix the Blue Cheese crumbles and the Blue Cheese Dressing together lightly so as not to damage the crumbles and place inside the tomato.

Seasoned/Herbed Butter

See Flavored/Seasoned Butters for Preparing Croutons

Croutons

Spread bread slices heavily with seasoned Butter and cube. Place cubes on cookie sheet and toast in heated oven until crispy and brown. Serve with Stuffed Tomato Salad.

Filet Mignon En Croute

2 - 6 to 8 ounce Filet Mignons

Pie Dough for a 9 inch Pie

1 Tablespoon Cooking Oil

¼ cup chopped Onion

¼ cup chopped Green Onion- tips only

½ cup sliced Mushrooms

½ cup diced celery

Sauté above vegetables until just tender. Preheat oven to 350 degrees (very important step). Roll out pie dough, very thin, and cut into two circles. *Charcoal grill or broil filets until slightly rare* (meat will continue to cook in pastry in oven. When Filets are room temperature, place each on a circle of pie dough and top with the sautéed vegetables. Bring pastry to the top of each filet and pinch to seal. Invert the encrusted filets and place on baking sheet or seal each crust tightly and cut leaves from unused pie dough to decorate each crust top. Place on baking sheet and bake in preheated oven until crust is brown—approximately 15 minutes.

Grilled Mixed Vegetables

Yellow and Green Squash

Red, Yellow and Green Bell Peppers

Sliced White Onions

Teriyaki Sauce

Italian Dressing

Marinate Vegetables (cut into large serving pieces) in a mixture of Teriyaki Sauce and Italian dressing for several hours. Grill on hot Charcoal Grill to desired doneness and color and serve while warm.

Hershey's "Perfectly Chocolate" Chocolate Cake

CAKE

2 cups Sugar

1 ¾ cups Flour

¾ cup Hershey's Cocoa

1 ½ teaspoon Baking Powder

1 ½ teaspoon Baking Soda

2 Eggs

1 cup Milk

½ cup Vegetable Oil

2 Tablespoons Vanilla

1 cup Boiling Water

Frosting

1 stick (½ cup) Butter

2/3 cup Hershey's Cocoa

1 teaspoon Vanilla

3 cups Powdered Sugar

1/3 cup Milk

Heat oven to 350 degrees. Combine dry ingredients in large bowl. Add Eggs, Milk, Oil and Vanilla. Beat for 2 minutes on medium speed of mixer. Stir in boiling water. (Batter will be thin). Pour into two 9-inch greased and floured pans. Bake 30 – 35 minutes. Cool 10 minutes in pans. Remove from pans to wire rack. Cool completely. Frost.

For Frosting, melt Butter, stir in Cocoa and alternatively add the Powdered Sugar, Vanilla and Milk. Beat on medium speed to spreading consistency. Add more Milk if needed.

Cherry Pie Filling that has been thinned with a flavored liqueur may be used in lieu of frosting.

VALENTINE'S DAY DINNER FOR TWO MENU #2

Salad

Apple Spinach Salad
Mint Iced Tea

Main Course

Roast Leg of Lamb
Deep Fried Potato Cubes with Rosemary
and French Fried Onions
Steamed Asparagus with White Sauce
Hi Rise Yeast Rolls
White Zinfandel

Dessert

Strawberry Short Cake
Amaretto and Cognac

Apple-Spinach Salad

1 10-ounce package fresh baby Spinach

2 Apples (Granny Smith), peeled and diced

½ cup Cashews

1 cup sliced Mushrooms (fresh)

Optiona

½ cup Raisins or Craisins

¼ cup Sugar

¼ cup Apple Cider Vinegar

¼ cup Vegetable Oil

¼ teaspoon Garlic Salt

¼ teaspoon Celery Salt

Combine first four ingredients. Combine Sugar and next four ingredients in a jar – cover tightly and shake vigorously. Pour over Spinach mixture, tossing gently. Raisins or Cran-raisins (about ½ cup may be added). Yield: 6 servings.

Mint Flavored Iced Tea

Tea (loose or bags)

Sweetner (if desired)

Fresh Mint Leaves

Lime (if desired)

While tea is hot and steeping, press Mint (with back of spoon or fork) until mint leaf releases flavor and add to steeping tea. Tea may be pre-sweetened if desired . Add a slice/wedge of Lime for added flavor.

MARKET LIST: Boneless Leg of Lamb, Irish Potatoes, Parsley, Asparagus, Green and White Onions, Red Bell Pepper, Vegetable Oil, Crushed Red Pepper, Rosemary, Dijon Mustard, Milk, Butter, White Pepper, Fresh Berries, Strawberries or Raspberries ,Flour, Sugar, Lemon Juice, Vegetable Shortening, Yeast, Port Wine.

Roast Leg of Lamb

2-½ pound boneless Leg of Lamb

2 teaspoons Thyme

2 Tablespoons coarse Black Pepper

4-6 Tablespoons dried Rosemary

6-8 Cloves Garlic

Dijon Mustard

2 cups good Port Wine

2 cups Water (add more if needed during roasting)

Remove any bindings from Lamb, open and place three or four coarsely chopped Garlic cloves in the center, then tie with kitchen twine at one or two locations just to hold. Slit the Lamb at the thickest parts and insert several thickly sliced Garlic wedges. Place an approximate 18 inch strip of Aluminum Foil on a countertop and pour the spices on the foil and mix together. Spread Dijon Mustard all over the Lamb. Roll the Lamb in the spices. Pour the Port Wine and the water in the bottom of a roasting pan. Place the Lamb on a rack in the roasting pan. Roast partially covered with an aluminum foil tent at 350 degrees for 1-½ to 2 hours or until the meat thermometer indicates 175 degrees to 180 degrees. Remove foil tent during the last half-hour of roasting. Yield: 4 servings.

Deep Fried Potato Cubes with Fried Onions and Chives

2 pounds Baking Potatoes (about 4)

Peeled and cut into 1-½ inch cubes

½ teaspoon Sea Salt

1 ½ quarts cooking oil

1 large Onion, sliced and separated into rings

2 Tablespoons flour

Fresh ground Black Pepper

1 Scallion including green top, sliced

¼ red Bell Pepper, finely diced

¼ teaspoon dried Red Pepper Flakes

Put the Potato cubes in a large saucepan of salted water and add ¼ teaspoon of Sea Salt. Bring to a boil and cook until the Potatoes are so tender they're almost falling apart, 25-30 minutes. Carefully drain the potatoes and leave them to air-dry on a rack. When the Potatoes are cool enough to handle, arrange them in a single layer on two small, waxed-paper lined baking sheets. Wrap tightly with plastic wrap and freeze.

Shortly before serving, heat the oven to 200 degrees. In a deep fryer or medium saucepan, heat the oil over moderate heat to 325 degrees. Fry half the frozen potatoes until golden, about 15 minutes. Do not let them brown too fast. With a slotted spoon, transfer the potatoes to paper towels. Keep warm in the oven on a rack set on a baking sheet. Repeat with the remaining Potatoes.

Put the Onion rings in a medium bowl. Add the flour, the remaining ¼ teaspoon Sea Salt and 1/8 teaspoon Pepper and toss together. Fry in the hot oil until golden brown, about 10 minutes. Drain on paper towels. Sprinkle the Potatoes with Sea Salt and ¼ teaspoon Pepper. Scatter the Fried Onions, the Diced Red Bell Pepper and the Red Pepper Flakes over the top of the Potatoes and serve.

Steamed Asparagus with White Sauce

1 Bunch Fresh Asparagus	¾ to 1 cup Milk
2 Tablespoons Butter	Salt
2 Tablespoons Flour	White Pepper

In a small pot, bring water to boil. Place the Asparagus in a steam basket and place in the pot Steam until tender crisp.

WHITE SAUCE: Melt the Butter in a skillet. Add Flour, stirring constantly until smooth. Cook for 1 minute. Slowly add Milk, continuing to stir. Add a dash of white Pepper and 1/8 teaspoon of Salt. When the sauce is thickened, pour over the Asparagus and serve.

Hi Rise Yeast Rolls

6 cups all-purpose Flour	2 packages Yeast
2 cups sweet Milk	1 ¼ teaspoon Salt
½ cup Sugar	½ cup warm water
½ cup Shortening	

Scale Milk with Sugar and Shortening. Cool to lukewarm. Add Yeast to warm water, let stand for 5 minutes. Combine Milk mixture and Yeast in large bowl. Combine Flour and Salt. Beat in Flour gradually, knead Lightly. Return to bowl, cover with damp cloth. Let rise about 2 hours until dough doubles in size. Knead dough and form into three small balls and place in greased muffin tin. Allow to rise until each muffin tin is filled. Bake at 350 degrees for 15 to 20 minutes. Brush tops with Butter.

Old-Fashioned Strawberry Shortcake

Shortcake

2 cups flour

¼ cup granulated Sugar

3 teaspoons baking Powder

½ teaspoon Salt

½ cup Butter

Strawberry Topping

3 pints fresh Strawberries

¾ cup granulated Sugar

1 cup Heavy Cream

2 Tablespoons Confectioner's Sugar

¾ cup Milk

Preheat oven to 450 degrees. Lightly grease an 8 inch round baking pan. In large bowl, sift Flour, Sugar, Baking Powder and Salt. With pastry blender, cut in Butter until mixture resembles coarse cornmeal. Make a well in center of mixture. Pour in milk all at once; mix quickly with a fork, just to moisten flour. Do not over mix. Turn dough into prepared pan. With fingers (dipped in a little flour) lightly press dough evenly into bottom of pan. Bake 15 minutes or until golden and cake tester inserted in center comes out clean.

Meanwhile, make Strawberry Topping. Wash berries in cold water, drain. Reserve several nice berries for garnish. Hull and slice rest of berries. Add Sugar, mix well. With rotary beater, beat cream just until stiff. Gently stir in confectioner's Sugar.

Loosen edges of cooled cake (10 minutes) with knife and turn out on wire rack.Cut cake in half crosswise. Put bottom, cut side up, on serving plate. Spoon over half of sliced berries. Set top of cake in place, cut side down. Spoonrest of sliced berries over top. Mound whipped cream lightly in center. Garnish with whole Strawberries. Serve at once. Yield 9 servings.

MARKET LIST: Boneless Leg of Lamb, Irish Potatoes, Parsley, Asparagus, Green and White Onions, Red Bell Pepper, Vegetable Oil, Crushed Red Pepper, Rosemary, Dijon Mustard, Milk, Butter, White Pepper, Fresh Berries, Strawberries or Raspberries, Flour, Sugar, Lemon Juice, Vegetable Shortening, Yeast, Port wine, Apples, Fresh Spinach, Mushrooms, Flavored Tea, Whipping Cream, Amaretto and Cognac, Limes, Mint Leaves

ST. PATRICK'S DAY DINNER MENU

Appetizer

Fresh Vegetables with
Blarney Spinach Dip and Marinated Artichokes
Devilled Eggs
Olive, Tomato and Fresh Cucumber Salad

Main Course

Corned Beef and Cabbage
Sautéed Bacon and Onion
Irish Soda Bread
Beer of Choice

Dessert

Irish Whiskey Cake with Whiskey Frosting
Irish Coffee

Fresh Vegetables with Blarney Spinach Dip and Artichokes

Prepare Trays of Fresh Vegetables

Cauliflower, Carrots, Celery Sticks, Broccoli, and Surround with Devilled Eggs and serve with Spinach Dip

Spinach Dip

1 10 oz. package frozen chopped Spinach

1 cup Sour Cream

½ cup Miracle Whip

4 Green Onions, Chopped (Green stems only)

½ cup Fresh Parsley, chopped

Lightly season with Sea Salt and White Pepper

Place frozen Spinach in colander and thaw. Squeeze/press Spinach to remove liquid and dry on paper towels. Mix Sour Cream and Miracle Whip. Add remaining ingredients and mix well. Serve chilled.

Salad

Cherry Tomatoes, Ripe Pitted Green and Black Olives, Fresh Cucumber peeled and chopped in 1-1 ½ " cubes. Serve fresh and do not dress. Sprinkle with Sea Salt, mix together and serve with chopped and marinated Artichokes.

Devilled Eggs

Boil Extra Large Eggs in Salted Water until Centers are firm, cool. Peel and cut each Egg in half and remove the yellow to a medium mixing bowl. Refrigerate the Egg halves while the filling is prepared. Adjust filling ingredients as needed to fill all halves. Recommend the following proportions for one half dozen boiled and halved Eggs.

¾ cup chopped Sweet Pickles   ½ cup chopped Dill Pickles

½ cup Miracle Whip (add more Miracle Whip by Tablespoon if needed)

½ cup chopped white onion

2 – 4 Tablespoons yellow Mustard

Mash Egg Yolks with fork and add to above mixture. Season with Salt and Pepper to taste. Fill the Boiled Eggs with mixture and sprinkle tops with Paprika.

Corned Beef and Cabbage

1 Four Pound Corned Beef Brisket

6-8 Medium New Potatoes

6 small White Onions

1 – 2 Turnips, cut into large pieces

12 – 14 Baby Carrots

1 Large Green Cabbage, cut into wedges

1 can Beer

Salt, Pepper and 4 – 6 Chopped Cloves of Garlic

Brisket should be soaked in cold water in advance of cooking. Drain, place in large pot and cover with fresh cold water. Slowly heat to simmer (do not boil). Add seasonings and Beer. Cook slowly until meat is tender (2 – 3 hours). Add carrots, Onions, potatoes and Turnips and cook until vegetables are cooked through, but firm. Place the Cabbage Wedges on top of the Brisket and continue to cook – Cover and steam until Cabbage is just tender. Adjust seasonings to taste and serve with freshly grated Horseradish.

Sautéed Bacon and White Onion

Fry 1 lb. thick sliced bacon until crisp, add White Onion, sauté and serve with main course.

MARKET LIST: Cauliflower, Celery, Broccoli, Eggs, Spinach (frozen), Sour Cream, Miracle Whip, Extra Large Eggs, Yellow Mustard, Cherry Tomatoes, Green and Black Olives (pitted), New Potatoes, White and Green Onions, Turnips, Cabbage, Cucumber, Canned Marinated Artichokes, Sweet and Dill Pickles, Four pound Corned Beef Brisket, Raisins, Baking Powder, Flour, Sugar, Vinegar, Baking Powder and Baking Soda, Caraway Seed, Orange Juice, Irish Whiskey, Beer, Butter, Ground Cloves, Powdered Sugar, Brown Sugar, Garlic, Thick Sliced Bacon, Whipping Cream, Bacon, Wheat Flour, Orange, Brandy, Irish Cream Liqueur, Cointreau or other Orange Liqueur, Milk

Irish Soda Bread

In a large mixing bowl, mix the following ingredients

4 cups Whole Wheat Flour

1 teaspoon Baking Soda

1 teaspoon Salt

2 cups White Flour

1 teaspoon Cream of Tartar

Mix dry ingredients and make a well. Add 1 Cup Buttermilk. Stir well with wooden spoon.

Knead the dough on a lightly floured board and flatten. Place in a well oiled Cast Iron pan. Bake for 30 – 40 minutes until golden brown.

Irish Whiskey Cake

1 9 ounce box of Raisins	Pinch of Salt
2/3 cup Irish Whiskey	Pinch of Ground Cloves
1 ½ sticks Butter	1 teaspoon Baking Powder
3 Eggs	¾ cup Brown Sugar
¾ cups Flour	

Pre-soak Raisins in Whiskey. Cream Butter and Sugar until fluffy. Separate Eggs. Sift Flour, Salt, Cloves and Baking Powder into a bowl. Beat Egg Yolks into mixture one at a time, alternating between yolks and flour mixture. Gradually add Whiskey and Raisin mixture. Add remaining Flour mix. Beat Eggs until fluffy and fold into mixture.

Bake in 7" pan at 350 degrees for 1-½ hours. Frost with Irish Whiskey Cake Frosting when cool.

Irish Whiskey Cake Frosting

2 cups Powdered Sugar

1 Tablespoon fresh squeezed Lemon Juice

1/8 cup Irish Whiskey

Mix ingredients until desired consistency. Frost cooled cake.

Irish Coffee

½ cup chilled Whipping Cream

2 Tablespoons Cointreau or other Orange Liqueur

1 Tablespoon Powdered Sugar

½ cup Irish Cream Liqueur

¼ cup Irish Whiskey

¼ cup Brandy

3 cups strong hot Coffee

1 teaspoon grated Orange Peel

Make ahead and chill for 4-6 hours. Beat Whipping Cream, Cointreau and Powdered Sugar, cover and refrigerate.

In each of four 8 to 10 ounce Coffee mugs, pour 2 Tablespoons Irish Cream Liqueur, 1 Tablespoon Whiskey and 1 Tablespoon Brandy. Pour hot Coffee over the mix and top with a dollop of Whipped Cream. Sprinkle with grated Orange Peel. Serve immediately.

MARDI GRAS
MENU AND RECIPES FOR SEASONAL AND HOLIDAY FOODS

Mardi Gras Brunch

Shrimp and Crabmeat Quiche
Mixed Vegetable Salad with French Dressing
Mini Biscuits with Mint Jelly
Frozen Blender Mimosas

Dinner

Seafood Gumbo
Steamed White Rice
Cheesy French Bread
Sweet Unsalted Butter
Sauvignon Blanc
Kings Cake
Cinnamon Hot Tea

Late Night Supper

Jambalaya
Grilled Garlic Bread with
Grated Parmesan
Pecan Pie
Kalua and Coffee

Shrimp and Crabmeat Quiche

½ pound Cocktail Shrimp, peeled, deveined

1 cup White Crabmeat (if canned drained)

Small White Onion, chopped fine

½ Green Bell Pepper, chopped fine

8-10 oz. Package Grated Cheddar Cheese

4 medium Eggs, Beaten

¼ cup Butter

1 cup Milk

½ cup Evaporated Milk

9 inch Baked Quiche Pie Shell

Saute Onions and Bell Pepper in Butter. Beat Eggs with Milk and add Cheese and all ingredients. Pour into baked pie shell and bake for 45 minutes until the filling rises and is cooked through.

Mixed Vegetable Salad with French Dressing

Slice and Serve the Vegetables on Chilled Salad Plates

Purple Onions
Ripe Tomato Slices
Bell Pepper Slices/Rings
Artichoke Hearts
Rose Radishes
Serve on a Bed of Leaf Lettuce
With French Dressing

Mini Biscuits with Mint Jelly

Prepare Commercial Biscuit Mix
According to package instructions
Roll out dough and cut into 1-½" rounds
Bake until Golden Brown and Crisp
Serve with a commercially available Mint Jelly and Fresh Mint Leaves

Frozen Blender Mimosas

1 8 oz tube of Frozen Orange Juice
Ice Cubes to fill blender jar approximately ¼ full
Blend until ice and Orange Juice are well blended
Add Champagne, stir and pour into chilled Glasses

Cheesy French Bread

1 8 oz package shredded Mexican

¾ cup Mayonnaise or Salad Dressing
1 ½ teaspoon Dried Parsley Flakes

1/8 teaspoon Garlic Powder
Blend Cheese   1 (16 ounces) loaf French Bread
(cut in half, horizontally)

Combine Cheese, Mayonnaise, Parsley, Garlic Powder, stirring well. Spread evenly on cut sides of bread, place on a baking sheet. Bake at 350 degrees for 15 to 20 minutes or until Cheese is melted and brad is lightly browned. Slice crosswise into 1-inch slices. Serve immediately.

Jambalaya

½ cup Vegetable Oil

1 2 ½ – 3 pound Chicken

2 pounds Smoked Sausage

(cut into 1- ½ " strips)

2-3 cups Chopped White Onion

1 /cup Chopped Bell Pepper

2 cups Chopped Celery

3-4 Cloves Chopped Garlic

4 cups Long Grain White rice

3 cans Chicken Stock (add additional water

    if needed)to completely cover

Season with Salt, Pepper and Ground Ceyenne

Pepper or Tony Cachere's Creole Seasoning to

    taste

Cut up and de-bone chicken, rinse and fry chicken in Vegetable Oil in large, heavy pot. Remove chicken and sauté Onions, Garlic, Bell Pepper and Celery in the same pot. When Onions are clear, add the Sausage, Rice, Chicken, and Creole Seasoning and the Chicken Stock. Stir all ingredients, cover, reduce heat to low and simmer until rice is done . Do not lift the lid for at least one hour.

Grandma Gray's Southern Pecan Pie

¼ cup Butter

2/3 cup Brown Sugar (firmly packed)

¼ teaspoon Salt

¾ cup Dark Corn Syrup

3 Eggs, beaten

1 teaspoon Vanilla

1 cup Pecan Halves

1 unbaked Pie Shell

Cream Butter and Sugar until fluffy. Add Salt, Syrup, Eggs and Vanilla. Sprinkle Pecans over Pastry, then pour filling over Pecans. Bake at 350 degrees for 40 minutes or until knife inserted in center comes out clean. Note: I use about 2 cups of Pecan Halves although her original recipe is as is. I also place the Pecan Halves on a cookie sheet, sprinkle with Sugar and toast about fifteen minutes in the oven at 350 degrees, cool, then sprinkle over Pastry Shell.

Flaky Pie Crust

2 cups Flour

¾ teaspoon Salt

2 teaspoons Sugar

2/3 cup solids hortening

3-4 Tablespoons Cold Water

Sift Flour, Salt and Sugar together. Cut in Shortening with a knife or pastry blender. Add water gradually and blend to make a dough. Turn the dough onto a floured surface, divide into two pieces and roll to 1/8" thickness. Makes two 8" pie shells. Fill one unbaked shell with Pecan mixture and roll second shell in plastic or waxed paper for second pie or other use.

Seafood Gumbo

½ cup Vegetable Oil or Bacon Drippings

1 cup Flour

1 bunch Green Onions

1 Green Pepper, diced

1 large White Onion, diced

3 stalks Celery, diced

2 cloves Garlic, minced

1 large tomato, chopped

2 quarts water

2 teaspoons pepper

¼ cup minced fresh Parsley

2 cups Water

1 ½ pounds unpeeled medium fresh Shrimp

1 pint large Oysters, not drained

1 (10 ounce) package frozen sliced Okra thawed

½ pound Crabmeat

Gumbo file

Hot Cooked Long Grain White Rice

1 ½ teaspoon Salt

½ teaspoon Red Pepper

Heat Vegetable Oil or Bacon Drippings in large Heavy Skillet over medium heat; stir in Flour.

Cook, stirring constantly, about 30 minutes or until roux is the color of Chocolate.

Slice Green Onions, reserving green tops and set aside. Cook sliced Green Onions, Green Pepper, Onion, Celery, Garlic and Tomato in Roux until vegetables are tender. Combine vegetables, 2 quarts water, and next 4 ingredients in a large Dutch oven, stir well. Simmer, uncovered, for 2 hours. Add 2 cups of water and bring to a boil.

Peel and devein Shrimp. Add Shrimp, Oysters, Okra and Green Onion tops. Simmer 10 minutes. Stir in Crabmeat and Gumbo File. Let stand 15 minutes. Add water, if necessary for desired consistency. Serve over White Rice. Prepare rice according to package directions.

Cinnamon Hot Tea

Brew Tea and steep for 10-15 minutes
Heat quickly and stir in desired Sugar and lemon juice
Stir with Cinnamon Sticks and serve hot with lemon wedges.

Grilled Garlic Bread With Grated Parmesan

3 Small Loaves of French Bread (approximately 12" in length)
½ cup Garlic Butter (Sweet Cream Butter mixed with3 whole cloves of fresh chopped Garlic
2 Tablespoons Paprika
3 Tablespoons chopped Fresh Parsley
½ cup grated Parmesan Cheese

Cut loaves diagonally and spread Garlic Butter onto each cut side. Sprinkle with Parsley and Paprika. Bake in hot oven for 5 minutes and then sprinkle with Parmesan Cheese and return to oven for an additional 3-5 minutes. Wrap in napkin and serve warm with bowls of Jambalaya.

King Cake

King Cake is a sweetened yeast dough cake with a history dating back to the Epiphany and representing the gift of a special cake in honor of the three Kings.. "A Kings' Cake". A year of good fortune awaits the lucky person who gets the little figure which is inserted inside the cake representing the Christ Child.

1/3 cup warm water in large bowl
2 packages dry yeast
Dissolve the yeast in the warm water and set aside

½ cup Milk

½ cup Sugar

½ teaspoon Salt

½ cup Butter

3 large Eggs, beaten

1 teaspoon Cinnamon

1 teaspoon grated Lemon Rind

4 – 5 cups all purpose Flour

Heat Milk, Sugar, Butter and Salt until Butter melts, cool and add to yeast mixture. Stir in 2 cups of flour and mix well. Add 2 more cups of flour and mix until smooth and pliable. Continue working the flour into the dough until smooth. Flour a smooth surface and knead the dough five to ten minutes. Place the dough in a large greased bowl and place in a warm area until the dough rises approximately double. Punch down and knead again. Divide the dough into 3 equal parts and roll into a rope about 30 inches long. Braid the dough lengths and form into a circular cake. Seal the ends of the braids together and let the cake rise. Put the "baby" plastic figure beneath one of the braids and push into the dough. Bake until browned, prepare the glaze by mixing 2 cups Powdered Sugar with 1 Tablespoon each of warm water and lemon juice. Spread glaze over cooled cake and sprinkle with granulated Sugar using gold, green and purple food coloring to color approximately 3 equal sections of the cake.

MARKET LIST: Vegetable Oil and Solid Shortening, Flour, Sugar, Tea, Green and White Onions, Celery, Green Peppers, Garlic, Tomatoes, Frozen Okra, Oysters, Chicken, Smoked Sausage, Creole Seasoning, Parmesan Cheese, Grated Cheddar Cheese, Butter, Parsley, Shrimp, Chicken Stock, Milk, Sugar, Lemon, Long Grain White Rice, Vanilla, Tony Cachere's Cajun Seasoning, Eggs, Vanilla, Corn Syrup, Cinnamon and Cinnamon Sticks, Kalua, Paprika, French Loaves of Bread, Crabmeat, Gumbo File, Yellow, Purple and Green Food Coloring, Pecan Halves (remove those items from the list for recipes you do not plan to make from this section).

EASTER SUNDAY MENU #1

Appetizer
Flo's Quiche
Blender Mimosas

Main Course
Smoked Ham with Brown Sugar, Pineapple and Clove Crust
Green Cabbage Slaw
Baked Sweet Potatoes with Marshmallow/Pecan Dressing
Doubly Good yeast Rolls
Apricot Tea

Dessert
Fresh Apple Cake
Coffee

Your family can begin this special holiday with Quiche and Mimosas and enjoy a casual lunch of Smoked Ham (which they have taste-tested extensively) with delicious accompaniments. And, "real men" not only eat my quiche –some have threatened to ransack the freezer to get to those already prepared and frozen or have even asked nicely for one of those "pie things" you make. They are so good and you can change the recipe to include any favorite substitute.

Flo's Quiche

6-8 slices Bacon

½ cup grated Swiss Cheese

3 Green Onions, chopped

¼ teaspoon Salt

¼ teaspoon Nutmeg

Dash Cayenne Pepper

1 ½ Tablespoons Flour

2 cups Light Cream

4 Eggs slightly beaten

1 unbaked Pie Crust

Prepare Pie Crust and place in floured/dusted quiche pan or 9" pie plate. Cook bacon until very crisp. Crumble. Sprinkle Bacon, Cheese and Onion into Crust. Using a 4 cup measure or medium mixing bowl, mix Salt, Nutmeg, Cayenne Pepper, Flour together and gradually stir in Milk. Blend together well. Beat Eggs in medium mixing bowl and slowly stir mixture into Eggs. Mix and pour into crust. Bake at 350 degrees for 35 – 40 minutes until firm in center. This recipe is very versatile and the following are additions or substitutions you may wish to try. Add Frozen Spinach (thaw, chop, press dry) and combine with bacon, cheese and onion. Add sliced Mushrooms, substitute cooked Italian Sausage for Bacon, substitute Crabmeat and Cocktail Shrimp for Bacon, add Chopped and well drained Broccoli to Cheese and Onion. The additions may require additional cooking time.

Blender Mimosas

Crushed Ice

Orange Juice

Champagne

Orange Slices

Mint Sprigs

Crush Ice in blender. Fill each glass approximately ½ full of crushed ice. Mix Champagne and Orange Juice in a large pitcher and pour over Ice. Serve with Orange Slices and garnish with a Sprig of Mint.

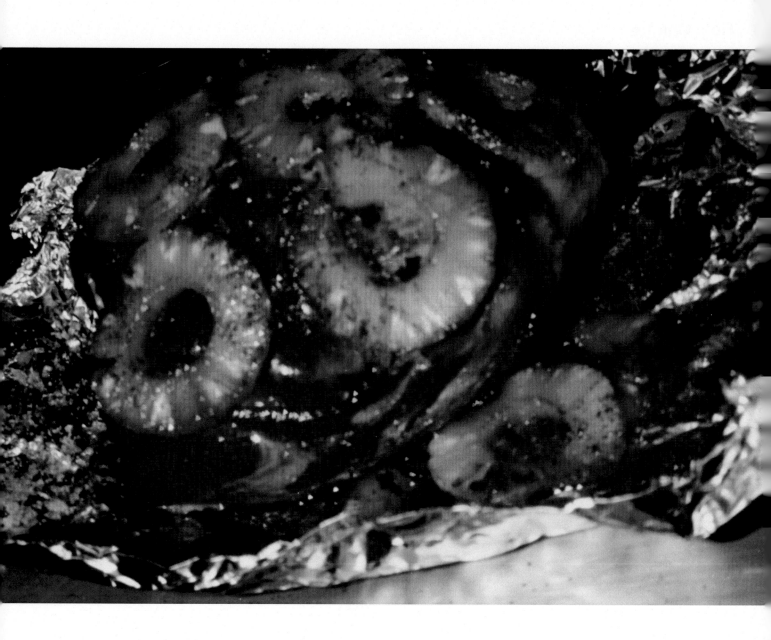

Smoked Ham with Brown Sugar, Pineapple and Clove Crust

Purchase whole, Sugar or salt cured Ham (do not use Circle Cut). Begin boiling the Ham out in a large roasting pan the night before. Fill the roasting pan approximately half full of water, place the ham in the water and bring to a boil. Reduce the temperature, turn the ham several times in the water to cover all sides. Empty the water and replace with fresh hot water once or twice more, heat to a boil, reduce heat and allow to cook for an additional 20-30 minutes more. Remove Ham from water, rinse with clean water, place on a double wrapper of heavy Aluminum foil. Cool and refrigerate.

1 can of Sliced Pineapple (drained)

2 cups Brown Sugar
¼ cup of Whole Cloves

Open aluminum wrapped Ham and place Pineapple Slices on Ham to cover and secure with toothpicks. Press whole cloves into the skin of the Ham randomly and in the center of the Pineapple Slices. Sprinkle Brown Sugar generously over the Ham and close the foil cover.

Prepare a Mesquite Chip and Charcoal Bar B Q fire. To insure smoke flavor, place chips in metal pan over charcoal and frequently sprinkle with water. Place the Ham on the grill (not directly on the fire). Cook for one hour then open the Foil Wrap. Cook for another hour and half, checking frequently to prevent excessive browning of the Pineapple Slices. If needed, place a loose foil cover to prevent over-browning.

Cabbage Slaw

4 cups Green Cabbage, Shredded

½ cup Celery, finely sliced

1/3 cup Green Pepper, chopped

¼ cup Sweet Red Pepper, chopped

2 Green Onions, chopped fine

¾ cup Sour Cream

3 Tablespoons Vinegar

3 Tablespoons Sugar

1 teaspoon Salt

Or finely sliced Carrot   sprinkling of White Pepper

1 teaspoon Celery Seed

Combine Cabbage, Celery, Peppers and Onions. Combine remaining ingredients; pour over Cabbage mixture. Mix/toss gently.

N O T E : I like to chill this slaw about an hour before serving. It can be beautifully presented by coring out a large green or purple cabbage with large, undamaged leaves from which you remove the center and fill with this mixture. Cabbage Slaw can be presented/served on a bed of shredded Lettuce or served in Red or Green Bell Peppers.

Baked Sweet Potatoes with Marshmallow/Pecan Dressing

Select medium size and well-rounded Sweet Potatoes. Scrub and bake potatoes until crisp outside and soft to the squeeze.

Prepare the Dressing while Potatoes are roasting.

1 cup Brown Sugar

½ stick Butter

½ cup Sugar

½ bag of White Miniature Marshmallows – 2 – 3 cups

½ cup White Corn Syrup

1 Tablespoon Vanilla

1 cup Chopped Pecans or Walnuts

Melt Marshmallows in a medium sized pot on low heat, stirring constantly. Add Sugar, Brown Sugar, Butter and Corn Syrup. Stir and cook until all ingredients are melted and mixture is thick and clear—bring to a boil, then reduce heat. Add Vanilla and Pecans or Walnuts. Serve in a candle-heated or canned heat small server as a dressing for the Roasted Sweet Potatoes. Potatoes can be spread in a casserole dish and covered with this dressing. Keep warm and serve in heated dish.

Doubly Good Yeast Rolls

1 teaspoon Sugar

1 teaspoon Salt

1 package Dry Yeast

½ cup Water

2 Eggs

7 cups all purpose Flour

½ cup Sugar

1 cup Shortening

2 cups Water

Combine first five ingredients in a mixing bowl; mix two minutes on low speed, set aside. Combine Flour and remaining ingredients in a large mixing bowl, mix 3 minutes with a heavy-duty mixer at medium speed. Add yeast mixture, mix 3 minutes at medium speed. Cover and let rise in a warm place (85 degrees) about 3 hours or until double. Punch down, cover and refrigerate overnight. With lightly floured hands, shape dough into 1-1/2 inch balls, place balls in 2 or 3 greased 9 inch round pans. Let dough rise in a warm place (85 degrees) for 2 hours or double. Bake @ 400 degrees for 10-12 minutes.

NOTE: Dough may be stored in refrigerator for up to four days.

Fresh Apple Cake

3 cups Flour

2 cups Sugar

1 teaspoon Soda

½ teaspoon Salt

1 teaspoon Cinnamon

2 Tablespoons Vanilla

2 Eggs (well beaten)

1 cup Salad Oil

3 cups Chopped Apples

1 cup Chopped Pecans or Walnuts (nuts optional)

Beat 2 Eggs well – set aside. Peel, core and chop 3 – 4 Red Delicious Apples – set aside. In large mixing bowl, sift dry ingredients and make a well. Add liquids (do not use mixer) and mix well. Add Apples and Nuts. Stir gently and spoon into a greased and floured tube or Bundt pan. Bake 1 hour to 1 hour and 15 minutes at 325 degrees. Turn and cool on a rack. Allow cake to cool and dry and serve with whipping cream or ice cream.

MARKET LIST: Ham, Canned Pineapple, Brown Sugar, Whole Cloves, Cinnamon, Apples, Sugar

EASTER SUNDAY MENU #2

Appetizer

Almost Shrimp Paesano
Baked Crisp Italian Bread Slices
Chilled Pinot Grigio

Main Course

Roasted Rock Cornish Game Hens
Sweet Corn (on the cob) with Seasoned Butter Sauces
Potato Salad
All Bran Refrigerator Rolls
Iced Tea

Dessert

Homemade Peach Freezer Ice Cream

This menu is a collage which includes the "best guess" recipe for a favorite Shrimp dish served in a San Antonio, Texas, restaurant named Paesano's (prepared repeatedly until we achieved this "almost" recipe). I recommend you serve it with Baked Crisp slices of Italian Bread and a well chilled Pinot Grigio.   I hope you enjoy it and the other family favorite summer-time and picnic Potato Salad and Corn on the Cob.

Almost Shrimp Paesano

12 – 18 Medium Raw Shrimp

1 Quart Half and Half

3 Cups all purpose Flour

¼ - ½ cup Wesson Oil or Olive Oil

2 large Egg (Yolk only)

1 stick Unsalted Butter

2-3 Cloves Fresh Garlic, Chopped Fine

½ cup Chopped Parsley

½ cup Lemon Juice

Shell, devein and remove head of Shrimp. Place in deep glass dish, pour half of the cream over the Shrimp, cover and soak in refrigerator overnight.

Make the Sauce: Gently beat egg yolks with Lemon Juice and Butter and stir over low heat until Butter is melted. Continue to heat and stir and add ½ cup Half & Half and chopped Parsley and Garlic and remove from heat when sauce has thickened.

Remove Shrimp from cream, drain and roll shrimp in flour.

Sauté shrimp in oil over medium heat until partially cooked. Do not overcook. Do not turn shrimp. Remove to baking dish (keeping cooked side down) or individual baking/serving dishes and place in preheated oven. Set oven to Broil and broil Shrimp until crisp and cooked through. Place small amount of sauce over Shrimp and serve crisp sides up with remaining sauce and toasted slices of Seasoned Italian Bread.

Roasted Rock Cornish Game Hens

Clean two Cornish Game Hens and remove necks and gizzards. Place Hens chest side up in a roasting pan. Mix the following ingredients and stuff in the cavity of each Hen and spread mixture generously over and around Hens before roasting. Cover with aluminum foil for first 15 – 20 minutes of roasting. Bake in a 350 degree oven and doneness will register 185+ on the thermometer. Double the vegetable mixture and Chicken Broth for four Hens.

One large White Onion, chopped

One bunch Green Onions, cleaned and chopped

One Red Bell Pepper, seeded and chopped

One Green Bell Pepper, seeded and chopped

3-4 large sticks Celery, chopped

3-4 cups sliced Mushrooms

Add ½ can Chicken Broth

Mix and sprinkle over Birds

2 teaspoons Ground Sage

1 teaspoon Paprika

Sea Salt and fresh ground Black

Pepper

Sea Salt and fresh ground Black Pepper

SWEET CORN (ON THE COB) WITH SEASONED MELTED BUTTERS

Shuck and clean (remove all silks) one ear of Sweet Corn for each guest. Place in a large pot of hot, salted water with generous amount of Butter and boil until corn is tender and turns a shining, golden color. Reduce heat, leave Corn in hot water until just before serving, drain in colander. Prepare Seasoned Butters.

PAPRIKA BUTTER SAUCE

Melt two sticks of Butter in sauce pan. Mix together 1 teaspoon Sea Salt; ½ teaspoon ground White Pepper; ½ teaspoon Paprika; ½ teaspoon Tarragon; 1 teaspoon Oregano. Heat until blended and transfer to a candle warming server to be served as an accompaniment to Corn.

CRUSHED RED PEPPER/GARLIC BUTTER

Melt two sticks of Butter in sauce pan. Mix together 1 teaspoon Crushed Red Pepper; 1 teaspoon finely chopped fresh Garlic cloves; 1 teaspoon Sea Salt; ½ teaspoon fresh ground Black Pepper. Heat until blended, adjust seasonings to taste, serve as an accompaniment/dipping Butter for Corn.

Sweet Corn is such a flavorful and enjoyable vegetable and can be prepared and presented in a variety of dishes or alone with Butters and seasonings. Corn is easily removed from cob by standing corn on large end and slicing kernels from the cob with a sharp knife. Corn can be cooked by seasoning and roasting in the husk after removing silks and replacing husk, securing with kitchen twine and offered at a variety of casual, picnic and outside events with Butter dip and a variety of shakers of salt and seasonings.

Potato Salad (Easter Bunny)

8 medium-sized Russet Potatoes, peeled

¾ cup white Onion, diced medium

2-3 Celery stalks from center of bunch, sliced thin

¾ cup Polish Dill Pickles, chopped

1 cup sweet Pickles, chopped

½ bunch Green Onions, sliced

½ to ¾ cup roasted Red Pepper or Pimento in oil, chopped

¾ cup Miracle Whip (more if needed to bind salad)

Sea Salt and fresh ground Black Pepper to taste

Peel the Potatoes and chop into 1 to 1 ½ inch squares. Boil in salted water until just done. Do not overcook. Drain the Potatoes and combine with all other ingredients. Mix well. Place on a serving platter and garnish as desired. Chill and serve. Note: For this meal, I formed the salad into a Rabbit using a wreath of fresh edible flowers around the neck and tail. I placed Parsley around the outside edges to resemble grass, then sliced a stuffed Green Olive in half for the eyes. Whiskers were made out of thinly sliced Green Onions and an edible Pink Carnation made a nose. Green Bell Peppers were cut to resemble ears.

All-Bran Refrigerator Rolls

1 cup Shortening

2/3 to ¾ cup Sugar

1 cup All Bran Cereal

1 ½ to 3 Tablespoons Salt

1 cup boiling water

2 Eggs, well beaten

2 cakes or 2 packages dried Yeast

1 cup lukewarm water

6 to 6 ½ cups Flour

Combine Shortening, Sugar, All Bran and Salt. Add boiling water, stir until Shortening is melted. Cool, add Eggs and Yeast softened in lukewarm water. Add 3 cups Flour and beat well. Add remaining Flour, beat well. Knead on floured board. Place in greased bowl, cover and let rise about one hour. Bake for 20 minutes in 350 – 400 degree oven.

You may refrigerate after kneading and mixture will keep for 3-4 days in sealed plastic bag in refrigerator. To bake after refrigeration, remove from refrigerator, place in greased bowl for 1 ½ to 2 hours, roll, cut into desired shape, allow to rise another 45 minutes to 1 hour, then bake in 350   400 degree oven for 20 minutes. This recipe yields 36 rolls.

Fresh Peach Homemade Ice Cream

6 cups ripe Peaches, peeled, seeded, chopped

3 ½ to 4 cups Sugar

Dash of Salt

2 Tablespoons all purpose Flour

4 cups whole Milk

1 cup heavy Cream

1 12 oz. can evaporated Milk

6 Large Eggs, beaten

2 Tablespoons Vanilla Extract

Place chopped Peaches and 1 cup of Sugar in food processor and pulse until Peaches are chopped fine. Do not process to puree stage. Mix together remaining Sugar, Salt and Flour in a large stock pot. Add Milk, Cream, Evaporated Milk and beaten Eggs to make the Custard. Cook and stir constantly over medium heat until Custard becomes thickened. Remove from heat and allow to cool. Stir in Peaches and Vanilla Extract and pour into a 5 quart electric freezer. Prepare freezer according to manufacturer's instructions using crushed ice and rock salt if directed. When freezer cuts off, ladle out any salt water, carefully remove paddle, add ice and pack ice cream for about an hour. To preserve ice cream, spoon into plastic containers and fill to the top to avoid collection of air and formation of crystals. Place in your freezer's coldest section.

There are a variety of Ice Cream Makers on the market currently and in a variety of sizes and types of freezing processes. This recipe is tested and used in the one gallon electric freezer which uses crushed ice and rock salt to freeze the custard. The above recipe requires that the custard be "cooked" as would be advised in any recipe incorporating raw eggs into the mix.

MARKET LIST: 1 ½ dozen raw Shrimp, Italian Bread Loaf, Evaporated Milk, Whole Milk, Cream, Eggs, Peaches, Vanilla Extract, All Bran Cereal, Yeast, Flour, fresh Sweet Corn, Sea Salt, Rock Salt, Paprika, Sweet and Dill Pickles, Red and Green Bell Peppers, Green and White Onions, Potatoes, Miracle Whip, Stuffed Olives, Pimento, Lemon Juice, Butter, Half and Half, Rock Cornish Game Hens, Pinot Grigio, Celery, Crushed Red Pepper, Black Pepper, Mushrooms, Ground Sage, Chicken Broth, White Pepper, Oregano, Tarragon, Fresh Edible Flowers, Parsley Sprigs, Tea Bags

EASTER SUNDAY MENU #3
SUNDAY BRUNCH

Appetizer

Shrimp and Crab Meat Puff Pastries
Chilled Ali Mosa Alize with Mint Sprigs, Orange and Lime Slices

Main Course

Fried Pork Loin
Grilled Smoked Sausages
Cream Cheese and Sour Cream Scrambled Eggs
Connally Congealed Salad
Angel Biscuits and Honey Butter

Dessert

Orange Blossom Cake
Coffee

Connally Congealed Salad

1 large box Cherry or Strawberry Gelatin

1 12-ounce can frozen Orange Juice
Concentrate

1 pint Whipping Cream

½ cup Sugar

1 cup finely chopped Celery

2 cups peeled, grated Apple

1 cup grated Carrots

1 cup finely chopped Pecans

1 ½ cup Miniature Marshmallows

Follow instructions on box for Gelatin, using only 2 cups hot Water. (Orange Juice and Whipping Cream replace 2 cups of cold Water). Beat the Whipping Cream with ½ cup Sugar until it reaches stiff peaks. Fold Orange Juice concentrate and Whipped Cream into the Gelatin. Add Celery, Apples, Carrots, Pecans and Marshmallows. Stir to distribute into the liquid mixture.

Prepare a gelatin mold by spraying with a non-stick spray or rubbing Mayonnaise on sides. Place mixture in mold. Chill until firm or overnight. Unmold and serve immediately. Salad can be prepared up to two days ahead.

NOTE: This is a delicious and treasured recipe which I have served at many special events and celebrations over the years. It was given to me by Mr. & Mrs. D. W. Hicks of Bandera, Texas, friends and business partners in the 70s. Mrs. Hicks was the sister of John B. Connally, Governor of Texas at the time, and this delicious recipe was a family favorite, hence the name Connally Congealed Salad.

Shrimp and Crab Meat Puff Pastries

Puff Pastry Shells

1 cup Water

½ cup Butter

Dash of Salt

1 cup Flour

3 Eggs

Bring 1 cup of Water, ½ cup Butter and a dash of Salt to a boil. Remove from heat. Add 1 cup of sifted Flour and beat with electric mixer until smooth. Add Eggs one at a time, beating after each addition. Drop mixture by rounded Tablespoons onto lightly greased baking sheet. Bake in pre-heated oven at 400 degrees for 8 to 10 minutes until puffed. Reduce heat to 350 degrees and bake until crisp and golden about 30 minutes. Remove and cool on rack. Using very sharp knife, cut a circular opening on top of each puff, remove any doughy membrane. Allow to remain open and dry until ready to fill with desired filling and serve promptly.

Shrimp and Crabmeat Filling

1 to 1 ½ pounds raw, peeled, deveined Medium Shrimp, heads removed	1 16 ounce package mild shredded Cheddar Cheese
2 cans Crabmeat, large lump	1 12 ounce package grated Velveeta Cheese
1 cup chopped Celery (include green leaves)	
1 cup chopped Green Onions	1 can sliced Water Chestnuts (drained)
½ cup chopped White Onions	Dash Crushed Red Pepper
1 large can Campbell's Cream of Mushroom Soup	Salt and Pepper to taste
	2 Tablespoons Olive Oil
1 Jar sliced Mushrooms	2 Tablespoons Canola Oil

In a large skillet, heat Olive and Canola Oil, add Onions and Celery, sauté until just tender, and add Mushrooms, Water Chestnuts and Shrimp, sauté until heated through. Pour Ceram of Mushroom Soup over sautéed mixture and heat thoroughly. Sprinkle Crushed Red Pepper, Salt and Pepper into mixture and adjust to taste. Stir in Velveeta Cheese and one half of the grated Cheddar Cheese, cook and stir over low heat until cheese is melted and mixture is thick. Drain and add Crabmeat, heat and stir gently to avoid separating the lumps of Crabmeat. Bring mixture just to a boil and remove pan from burner.

Prepare Puff Pastries, core and retain pastry caps. Fill prepared pastries with mixture, sprinkle remaining Cheddar Cheese on top, cover with pastry cap and serve immediately.

This recipe makes 12 to 14 servings as an appetizer. To prepare as main course, prepare larger puff pastry shells. Fill with mixture, top with Cheddar Cheese and serve with Green Salad or your choice of vegetables. Makes 6 generous main course servings.

Fried Pork Loin and Grilled Smoked Sausage Links

These dishes are so easily prepared and consume very little of your time on a busy Easter Morning. The Pork Loin is the Pork Tenderloin. Buy it whole, unseasoned, slice it in approximately ¾ thickness.

Pork Tenderloin with Brown Gravy

Heat Vegetable Oil in a shallow frying skillet. Salt and Pepper the Pork slices and dredge in White Flour. Fry the Loin slices to golden brown, turn and fry the other side. Do not overcook. The meat will be tender and ready to serve in under 10 minutes.

Note: I like to make a Brown Gravy with the drippings. Return the skillet to the burner, add a Tablespoon of Flour, season with Salt and Pepper and stir continuously until Flour is browned. Remove from heat briefly. Mix ½ cup whole Milk and ½ cup water and stir into Gravy base. Stir and cook to correct thickness. Add more liquid as desired.

SMOKED SAUSAGES

The Sausages presented in this book are Beef Sausages made by a famous meat company in Texas. However, Beef, Pork, Deer and Turkey, and combinations of these meats plus a variety of other Sausage fillings are available commercially in most super markets. The ones shown here are "smoked" (fully cooked) by the Sausage maker and are placed on a hot charcoal grill about 30 minutes before serving. You will want to rotate them frequently to avoid over-cooking or burning on one side.

Cream Cheese and Sour Cream Scrambled Eggs

1 16 ounce container of Sour Cream	1 8 ounce package Cream Cheese
12-18 Eggs	¾ cup Whole Milk
1 stick of Butter (melted)	Salt and Pepper to taste
1 cup Mild Cheddar Cheese, grated	

In blender, mix Sour Cream and Cream Cheese until creamy. Whip Eggs, add Milk and ½ of melted Butter. Salt and Pepper Eggs. Beat Egg mixture into Cream Cheese mixture. Place remaining Butter in non-stick skillet, add Egg and Cheese mixture and cook and stir until cooked through. Place in chafing dish, sprinkle with grated Mild Cheddar and serve warm.

Angel Biscuits

1 package Active Dry Yeast
2 Tablespoons warm Water
(105-115 degrees)
1 stick Butter, melted
5 cups self-rising Wheat Flour

¼ cup Sugar
½ teaspoon Baking Soda
1 cup Solid Vegetable Shortening
2 cups Buttermilk

Dissolve Yeast In warm water and set aside. Grease a 15 X 10 inch baking pan or cookie sheet with melted Butter. Stir together Flour, Sugar and Baking Soda. Cut in Shortening until dough makes balls about the size of peas. Mix Buttermilk with Yeast mixture. Add to Flour mixture and stir with a fork until moistened. Roll out to ½ to ¾ thick on a floured surface. Cut Biscuits with a 2 inch cutter. Place close together on prepared pan, cover with a damp cloth and allow to rise 1 hour. (Dough will not be doubled in size).

Bake in a 400 degree oven 15 to 20 minutes or until browned. Brush tops with melted Butter and serve hot. This recipe yields approximately 30 biscuits.

Orange Blossom Cake

½ cup Butter, softened
2 cups Sugar
7 large Eggs, separated
3 cups sifted Cake Flour
1 Tablespoon Baking Powder
¼ teaspoon Salt

½ cup Orange Juice
½ cup Water
1 Tablespoon Vanilla Extract
Orange Glaze
Candied Orange Zest

Beat Butter at medium speed with electric mixer about 2 minutes or until creamy. Gradually add Sugar, beating 5 – 7 minutes. Beat Egg Yolks lightly and add to Butter mixture, beating until blended. Combine Flour, Baking Powder and Salt and add to Butter mixture alternately with Orange Juice and Water, beginning and ending with Flour mixture. Beat at low speed with an electric mixer until blended after each addition. Stir in Vanilla.

Beat Egg Whites at high speed with an electric mixer until foamy, reduce speed to medium, and beat until stiff peaks form. Fold egg white into batter, spoon batter into a greased and floured 12 cup Bundt pan or 10 inch tube pan.

Bake at 350 degrees for 35 to 40 minutes or until a wooden pick inserted in center comes out clean. Immediately place pan on a double layer of damp cloth towels; press towels around sides of pan, and let stand 10-15 minutes. Remove cake from pan and cool completely on wire rack. Spoon Orange Glaze over cake; top with Candied Orange Zest.

Yield: 1 (10-inch) Cake

N O T E : See Orange Glaze and Zest instructions on next page (page 91).

Orange Glaze

2 large Oranges

2 cups Sugar

1 Tablespoon Cornstarch

1/3 cup Lemon Juice

8 Egg Yolks, lightly beaten

½ cup Butter, softened

Squeeze Juice from Oranges, pour through a wire strainer into a 1 cup liquid measuring cup, straining out any seeds. Measure 1 cup Juice; reserve remaining Orange Juice for another use. Combine   Sugar and cornstarch in a small saucepan; add Lemon Juice and 1 cup Orange Juice, stirring well with a wire whisk. Cook over low heat, stirring until Sugar dissolves (about 10 minutes). Stir about ¼ of hot mixture into Yolks; add to remaining hot mixture stirring constantly. Cook over low heat, stirring constantly, ten minutes or until thickened. Remove from heat, add Butter, stirring until well blended. Cool, cover and chill.

Candied Orange Zest

2 large Oranges

1 cup Water

½ cup Sugar

additional Sugar (optional)

Remove Zest (orange part only) from Oranges, using a zester and being careful not to remove white pith. Cut Zest into 2 inch strips. Combine Water and Sugar in a small saucepan; cook over medium heat until boiling. Reduce heat to low; stir in Zest and cook mixture 15 – 20 minutes or until candy thermometer registers 220 degrees. Remove Zest strips from Syrup with a slotted spoon and spread on wax paper to cool. Sprinkle with additional Sugar, if desired.

MARKET LIST: Oranges, Sugar, Cornstarch, Lemons, Butter, Eggs, Flour and Cake Flour, Orange Juice, Active Dry Yeast, Baking Soda, Vegetable Shortening, Buttermilk, Self rising Wheat Flour, Eggs, Cream Cheese, Mild Cheddar Cheese, Milk, Pork Loin, Smoked Sausages, Apples, Cherry or Strawberry Gelatin, Miniature Marshmallows, Pecans, Carrots, Celery, Whipping Cream, Orange Juice Concentrate, Limes, Alize, Mint Sprigs, Shrimp, Fresh or canned Crab Meat, Honey, Sour Cream, Green and White Onions, Cream of Mushroom Soup, Mild Grated Cheddar Cheese, Grated Velveeta Cheese, Water Chestnuts, Olive Oil and Canola Oil, Canned Sliced Mushrooms

CINCO DE MAYO CELEBRATION

Menu #1

Entremeses
Tray of Crisp Fried Tortilla Chips with
Salsa Mexicano, Salsa Verde, Guacamole Salad
Sangria

Main Course
Beef and Chicken Grilled Fajitas
Served with Sour Cream
Pico de Gallo
Grilled Chilies and Onions
Refried Beans
Spanish Rice
Flour Tortillas
Cerveza

Dessert
Flan Supreme
Café de Olla con Leche

Fried Tortilla Chips

1 Package Corn Tortillas

Sea Salt

Vegetable Oil to Deep Fry

To fry tortillas to a crisp chip, first cut the Tortillas in half, then cut down the middle of each half producing four equal pieces from each Tortilla.

Heat Vegetable Oil in Deep Frying pot – sides of vessel should be deep and allow for 3 to 4 Tortillas to be fried at one time. Drop a Tortilla quarter in the hot oil and when it rises and bubbles in the oil, add 8 to 10 more tortilla squares. Have a paper or towel lined bowl available and lift the fried chips with a wire strainer to the bowl. Sprinkle with salt immediately. Continue to cook and salt until all Tortillas are fried.

Salsa Mexicano

6 Chiles Serranos, Seeded and Stems Removed

1 large bunch Cilantro, Remove and Discard Stems

Fresh Lime Juice

4 Large Ripe Red Tomatoes

1 Medium White Onion

2 Teaspoons Sea Salt

Chop Chiles, Tomatoes, Cilantro (leaves only) and Onion. Mix together and squeeze in juice from 2 fresh Limes. Sprinkle with Sea Salt.

Salsa Verde

12 fresh Tomatillos, washed, dried and chopped

1 large White Onion, peeled and chopped

4 Cloves Fresh Garlic, peeled and chopped

Cook together until Tomatillos are soft

Cool

Place in blender with 2 Jalapeno Peppers, seeded and chopped

1 and ½ cups chopped Cilantro

Blend until thick liquid texture

Guacamole Salad

3 ripe Avacados (Green or Black skin)

2 medium to large ripe Tomatoes

1 small white Onion or ½ large white Onion

1 Lime

1 fresh Jalapeno Pepper or 1 fresh Serrano Pepper

3 or 4 sprigs Cilantro – chopped

Salt and Pepper

Peel ripe Avacados and mash with a fork. Do not process in blender. Peel and chop ripe Tomatoes. Peel and chop small white Onion (chop fine). Seed and chop Pepper. Combine all ingredients and squeeze the juice of the Lime into the mix. Add Salt to taste and Pepper (if desired). Serve immediately.

Serve Guacamole as an Appetizer with fresh fried Corn Tortilla Chips or as a side dish with Carnitas, Tacos or Fajitas.

Pico de Gallo

1 bunch fresh Cilantro, chopped
    (large stems removed)

3 large ripe tomatoes, diced

1 large White Onion, chopped

2 cloves fresh Garlic, chopped fine

4 or 5 Jalapeno Chilies,
    seeded and diced

I Lime

Fresh Ground Sea Salt

Combine Cilantro, Tomatoes, Onions, Garlic and Chilies. Squeeze the juice of the Lime over the mix. Toss. Grind fresh Sea Salt over the mix and toss. Serve with Fajitas accompanied by a bowl of chilled Sour Cream, Salsa Verde and Grilled Onions and Peppers.

Fajitas - Beef and Chicken

There are a variety of good Fajita seasonings on your supermarket shelves today and meat markets in Texas often prepare and market a seasoning mix for Fajitas. I make the seasoning mix from "scratch" and admittedly do not "measure" carefully the various ingredients. The most notable variable is that I do not use Garlic Powder, but rather fresh garlic cloves which are chopped very fine. The seasoning mix below is adaptable for use with Chicken Breasts and Pork Tenderloin Fajitas. Avoid using the chili powder made from only one chili and select the traditional powder which blends a variety of dried chili and other spices.

2 Tablespoons Finely Chopped Garlic

(allow to dry - press between paper towels)

2 Tablespoons Ground Coriander

1 teaspoon Cayenne

1 Tablespoon Ground Cumin

1 Tablespoon Onion Powder

2 teaspoons course ground Black Pepper

1 Tablespoon Chili Powder

1 Tablespoon Fresh Ground Sea Salt

Clean, seed and prepare to cook

4-6 Pablano Peppers

2 each Red, Green and Yellow Bell Peppers

2 Large White Onions Split in half

Prepare a Charcoal Fire sufficient to cook all items including the Chicken Breasts (which will require approximately 30 -40 minutes depending upon the thickness) and the Beef Skirt Steaks (which will require 15-20 minutes depending upon thickness. Do not overcook. Grill Peppers and Onions. Remove from fire and place peppers in plastic bag. Allow to cool.

Rub spices on Chickens Breasts and place directly over hot coals on Charcoal Grill. Cook and turn until cooked through. Add Skirt Steaks and cook and turn frequently until cooked through. Remove both meats when done and place on wooden chopping board to debone and slice chicken and slice beef. Beef should be sliced on the diagonal. Keep warm. Remove skin from Grilled Peppers, cut into slices, separate cooked Onions into circles.

Heat a large Cast Iron Skillet or Tray in the oven to 500 degrees. Place sliced Chicken and Beef on the skillet, add Peppers and Onions, serve sizzling, accompanied by warm Tortillas, Sour Cream, Pico de Gallo and Salsas available for guests to select their choice.

Refried Beans

1 can refried beans

1 white Onion, chopped

2 cloves Garlic, chopped

½ tsp Crushed Red Pepper

½ stick unsalted Butter

Because processed and unseasoned Refried Beans are available in a variety of canned sizes, this is a very easy side dish. Brown Onion and Garlic together in Butter, add Red Pepper, stir and add Refried Beans. Heat over medium heat and stir continuously to prevent sticking to the pan. Serve immediately.

Spanish Rice

1 ½ cup White Long Grain converted white Rice

I large White Onion, chopped

1 large Green Bell Peppers, cored, seeded, chopped

3-4 cloves chopped fresh Garlic

1 ½ teaspoon Cumino Seeds

1 teaspoon Salt

1 cup Vegetable Oil

1 (large -28 oz) can Crushed
Tomatoes or tomato Sauce
with Tomato Bits

2 cups Water

½ teaspoon Black Pepper

Heat Vegetable Oil in large Cast Iron skillet. Add Rice, Onion, Bell Peppers, Garlic, Cumino Seeds and Salt and Pepper. Cook and stir on medium high heat until Rice and Onion are brown and peppers are translucent. Add small amount of oil if needed to sauté all ingredients.

When rice is brown and vegetables are cooked tender, add the Tomatoes. If whole canned Tomatoes are used, chop before adding to the skillet. Stir well and add water sufficient to cover all ingredients.Reduce heat, cover with tight fitting lid, and simmer at low temperature for 20 minutes without lifting lid, and until rice is cooked and all liquid is absorbed.

Sangria

(Recipe from the World's Fair, Spanish Pavilion, New York)

1 bottle (1 pint, 7 oz) Red Spanish Wine

2 ounces Cointreau

2 Tablespoons Sugar

2 ounces Spanish Brandy

1 Lemon, sliced

12 ounces Club Soda

½ Orange, sliced

24 ice cubes

Combine Wine, Sugar, Lemon and Orange slices in large pitcher. Stir until Sugar is dissolved. Add remaining ingredients. Let stand 15 – 20 minutes. Yield 4 tall glasses.

Flan Supreme

SAUCE

1 cup Sugar

Put Sugar in sauce pan and cook over low heat, stirring until melted and golden brown. Pour into mold and spread over the sides of the mold. This will harden, but will soften again when flan is cooking.

PUDDING

1 quart Milk or Half and Half

¾ cup Sugar

1/8 teaspoon (pinch) salt

1 teaspoon Vanilla

6 large Eggs, well beaten

In medium sauce pan, mix Milk, Sugar and Salt, boil vigorously for ten minutes. With electric mixer, beat mixture into the Eggs—a small amount at a time—beating continuously. Continue beating for 3 – 4 minutes to allow mixture to cool. Stir in Vanilla.

Fill a large pan approximately half full of hot water, place in the oven at a temperature of 300 degrees.

Pour mixture into the prepared mold and place mold in the water bath. Cook for 1 ½ hours or until knife inserted into Flan comes out clean. Allow to cool slowly, then refrigerate to chill completely. Unmold on a dish with raised edge in order to contain sauce.

Pour Brandy or Rum over Flan and light it just before serving.

Café de Olla (Coffee in a clay pot)

5 cups Water

½ cup Coarsly Ground Mexican

dark roasted Coffee

Peel of half an Orange

6-8 inches of stick Cinnamon

½ cup Sugar

5 Whole Cloves

Heat all but one cup of the water in a sauce pan. Bring to a boil, lower heat and add ground Coffee, Cinnamon Sticks, Cloves and Orange Peel. Simmer for 3-5 minutes and add remaining water. Remove from heat, cover and allow to steep. Strain seasonings and serve in clay mugs.

MARKET LIST: Dark Roast Coffee, Sugar, Stick Cinnamon, Cloves, Orange, Half & Half, Vanilla, Eggs, Garlic, Coriander, Cayenne, Cumin, Onion Powder, Chili Powder, Sea Salt, Pablano Peppers, Red, Green and Yellow Bell Peppers, White and Green Onions, Chicken Breasts, Beef Skirt Steaks, Tortillas, Refried Beans, Crushed Red Pepper, Unsalted Butter, Rice, Cumino Seeds, Tomato Sauce, Vegetable Oil, Spanish wine, Lemons, Oranges, Cointreau, Spanish Brandy, Club soda, Tomatoes, Lime Juice, Ripe Tomatoes, Eggs, Serrano Chilies, Cilantro, Avocados, Jalapeno Peppers, Tomatillos,

CINCO DE MAYO

Menu #2

Appetizer
Cheese Quesadillas with Salsa Verde
Taquitos de Puerco
Guacamole
Margaritas

Main Course

Jumbo Grilled Camarones
Cheesy Beef Enchiladas
Charro Beans
Warm Flour Tortillas with Butter and Sea Salt
Mexican Beer, Margaritas, Iced Tea

Dessert

Mexican Wedding Cake
(Also called Princess Cake)
Mexican Roasted Coffee con Leche

Cheese Quesadillas with Salsa Verde

One Package Corn Tortillas

1 8 ounce package grated Monterey Jack

    Or Mexican Four Cheese (2 cups)

1 cup Vegetable Oil for frying

Heat skillet with small amount of oil – to just cover bottom of pan. Set on low heat. Place first Tortilla in pan and cover with grated cheese, then cover with second Tortilla. Cook and turn until Tortillas are crisp and cheese has melted. Add vegetable oil as needed to continue to prepare additional Quesadillas. With large clever, cut Tortillas in half, then half again. Serve immediately with Green Salsa.

Note: See Salsa Verde recipe, Page 94

Taquitos De Puerco

Small Tacos with Pork

1 Pound of Boneless Pork (cut into 2" pieces)

Clove of Garlic

3-4 Peppercorns

½ teaspoon Salt

3-4 Cups Water

1 medium white Onion

1 small bunch Cilantro

15-20 Corn Tortillas

Vegetable Oil for frying Tortillas

Cook Pork in 3-4 cups of water seasoned with Garlic, Peppercorns and Salt. When Pork is tender, cool and shred the meat. Chop Cilantro and Onion and add to Pork. Salt to taste.

Prepare Taquitos by spreading a large tablespoon of meat mixture on each Tortilla. Tightly roll the Tortillas, secure with 2 toothpicks and cut each in half. Heat the Vegetable Oil and fry the Tortillas turning frequently until crisp and golden brown. Remove toothpicks and serve with Guacamole.

Note: See Guacamole recipe page 94

Margaritas

Probably no other single mixture identifies Mexican and South Texas celebrations more and more frequently than the Margarita. The story of it's origination in 1938 is that a bartender made a drink of Tequila and Mexican Limones in honor of a beautiful showgirl named Rita de la Rosa. There are many variations of this incredible drink and this book of celebrations presents this one for your personal pleasure – nicknamed "Margaritaville" (thank you Jimmy Buffet) begins with "Ice in the Blender" – 2 cups

1 cup Tequila

½ cup Triple Sec

8 oz can frozen Limeade (thawed)

Blend until frothy

2 Mexican Limes

Coarse Margarita Salt

Slice Limes and moisten tops of Margarita glasses

Dip top rim in Salt

Serve in Margarita glasses and garnish with Lime Slices

The original – made with French Orange Liqueur

One Cup of Cointreau Orange Liqueur

Two Cups Tequila

Juice of 4 or 5 Fresh Limes

Place in a Shaker and shake well, pour over ice in Margarita Glasses

Jumbo Grilled Camarones (Shrimp)

18 to 24 Jumbo (Texas) Gulf Coast Shrimp

    (quantity dependent upon number of guests)

½ pound block Mozarella Cheese

6 large Jalapeno Peppers

2 sticks Butter

Fresh Garlic, chopped medium/fine

Red and Green Bell Peppers

Large White Onions – cut in thirds

Clean, remove head, tail and devein Shrimp

Place Shrimp in container of Ice Water

Slice Mozarella into quarter inch slices

Seed and slice Jalapeno Peppers into quarter inch slices

Enlarge the deveining opening sufficient to place a slice of Mozarella Cheese and Jalapeno Pepper and into each Shrimp and secure with one or two toothpicks. Melt Butter and mix in finely chopped Garlic. When all Shrimp have been stuffed, place on a preheated Charcoal Grill, baste generously with Garlic Butter and Grill, turning frequently until Shrimp are cooked through and Cheese has melted. Do not overcook Shrimp.

Serve on a large platter in a bed of Cilantro Rice and Grilled Onions and Peppers.

Cheesy Beef Enchiladas

1 pound Ground Beef

2 10 ounce cans Enchilada Sauce

1 package Taco Seasoning

½ pound grated Mexican Four Cheese

½ pound grated Mozarella Cheese

12 Corn Tortillas

Vegetable Oil

1 medium Onion, chopped

Combine Cheeses and set aside. Brown Beef and pour off fat. Stir Taco Seasoning into beef. Fry each Tortilla quickly in hot oil, turning once. Stack in a warm place until all Tortillas have been fried. Fill each tortilla with small amounts of chopped Onion, cooked Beef and Cheese mixture. Roll and place seam side down in a casserole dish. Continue until all Tortillas are filled. Pour Enchilada Sauce evenly over Tortillas and top with Cheeses. Bake at 350 degrees for 15 – 20 minutes until Enchiladas are heated through and Cheese is bubbly and browned.

Charro Beans

1 16 oz. bag Pinto Beans (Frijoles Pintos)

½ teaspoon Cumin

1 large White Onion

½ teaspoon Chili Powder (optional)

1 lb. Salt Pork or Thick Sliced Bacon   Salt and Pepper to taste

2 Cloves Garlic

Water to soak – 4 cups

1 small bunch Cilantro, 10-12 sprigs, chopped   Water to cook – 4 – 6 cups

2 Jalapenos, seeded, chopped

2 Tomatoes, peeled, seeded

Water to cook – 4-6 cups

Pick over beans to remove soil or rocks. Rinse and drain. Place in large pot, cover with water and soak overnight. Pour water and beans into a collander, rinse beans and return to deep sided pot, add 4-5 cups of water and place on medium heat.

Add Salt Pork or Bacon, Garlic, Cumin, Chili Powder, Salt and Pepper. Cook uncovered on medium low heat and without stirring for approximately 2 ½ hours. Add water as needed. Test beans for doneness by removing a spoonful and mashing beans with back of a second spoon. When beans are just soft add chopped Onion, Jalapeno, Cilantro and Tomato. Stir only to add ingredients and continue to cook at low heat for an additional half hour or until beans are soft through. Adjust seasoning, serve as a side dish with Fajitas, Carnitas, Enchiladas or other Mexican entrees.

MARKET LIST: Flour and Corn Tortillas, Avacados, Tomatoes, White Onions, Monterey Jack Cheese, Pinto Beans, Tomatoes, Limes, Cilantro, Vegetable Oil, Garlic, Tequila, Triple Sec, Limeade, Margarita Salt, Jalapenos, Salt Pork or Bacon, Jumbo Shrimp, Block Mozarella Cheese, Butter, Red and Green Bell Peppers, Pablano Peppers, Long Grain Converted White Rice, Sugar, Flour, Vanilla, Crushed Pineapple, Powdered Sugar, Pecans (if desired), Cream Cheese, Strawberries, Kiwi, Fresh Pineapple, Cumin, Chili Powder

Mexican Wedding Cake

Also called the Princess Cake

This was a very popular lunch dessert aboard the Southern Empress, a riverboat paddlewheeler cruise ship, which I owned and operated for six years. Chef Sylvestre was the master of this often requested dessert by our guests and group charters. He dressed this cake with Kiwi, Pineapple Rings and Strawberries just before serving for a very pretty presentation.

2 cups Flour

2 cups Sugar

2 Tablespoons Baking Soda

2 Eggs, beaten

2 Tablespoons Vanilla

1 20 ounce can of Crushed Pineapple with Juice

Mix by Hand

Turn into a lightly greased and floured 9X13 Baking Dish

Bake for 35 minutes at 350 degrees

FROSTING

1 8 oz Cream Cheese at room temperature

1 stick of Butter

2 Tablespoons Vanilla

1 pound of Powdered Sugar

Mix with electric mixer until smooth and spread on warm cake

Add 1 ½ cups chopped Pecans to cake mix and place Pecan halves on frosting if desired. Cut into squares and serve with coffee.

JUNETEENTH FREEDOM CELEBRATION

Menu #1

Fried Chicken and Cream Gravy
Polk Salad Sautéed with Apple Cider Vinegar
Green Onions or chives
Roastin' Ears with Seasoned Butter Dips
Fried Yams
Skillet Corn Bread
Iced Tea, Beer

Cold Watermelon

This menu is designed around the family celebration in recognition of this important day in history. There is ordinarily no formal structure and much of the food preparation is shared between family members and friends. The foods featured here are "Southern" and reflect the great variety of tastes and interests of the participants and members of the family and attendees of events in celebration of this day.

Fried Chicken with Cream Gravy

The delicious "family style" fried chicken featured here bears little resemblance to the commercial fried chicken available at our "drive thru" chicken store. Ordinarily, the chicken is a broiler/fryer, often free range farm raised birds and once you taste the excellent flavors it is impossible to forget and not much else compares.

1 (3 pound) broiler-fryer, cut up

1-1/2 cup Flour

Salt and Pepper

1 cup Light Cream

1 cup Milk

Wash cut up chicken, pat dry with paper towels. In plastic bag, combine Flour, Salt and Pepper. Add Chicken pieces, a few at a time, shake until well coated. Pour Salad Oil to ½ inch depth in large "Chicken Fryer" sized skillet and heat slowly. Place larger pieces of floured chicken in fryer and heat slowly. Fry until golden brown. Reduce heat and cook, covered and turning occasionally for 30-35 minutes, or until tender. Remove cover and cook about 5 minutes longer, or until Chicken has a crisp exterior. Remove Chicken pieces to platter and keep warm. Chickens prepared depend upon number of guests.

To Make Gravy, heat remaining oil in skillet (including browned bits in bottom of pan), place two or three tablespoons of Flour in hot oil and season with Salt and Pepper.. Remove hot oil from heat, gradually stir in mixture of Light Cream and Milk to make a cream Gravy. Stir and cook until Gravy thickens to desired consistency. adjust seasonings and serve hot.

Sautéed Polk Salad with Apple Cider Vinegar

I first learned about this plant as a child visiting a friend after school whose parents sent her to pick the plant (which grows wild) to be included in the evening meal. The correct name of the plant is Poke Sallet and it is popular in the old South as a cooked 'vegetable' side dish. The plant was cooked and eaten during the great depression and earlier periods of severe food shortages and has remained on the Southern Table for generations. Poke Sallet grows wild and currently is available in North and East Texas, Oklahoma, Tennessee, Georgia, and other parts of the South. Only the young leaves of the plant should be harvested and cooked and the plant develops a poisonous character after about 18" of growth. Elvis Presley recorded the song "Polk Salad Annie" as did other Southern musicians of the seventies and eighties.

Pick the young, tender leaves of the plant

Remove stems and wash the leaves under running water

Place the leaves in small amount of water, parboil, rinse and repeat the procedure.

Place leaves in skillet with fried Bacon or cooked salt pork. Saute briefly – just till hot. Add Salt and Pepper and a Teaspoon of Apple Cider Vinegar. Serve with whole Green Onions or Green Onion bits.

Roastin' Ears with Seasoned Butter Dips

12 Ears Fresh Sweet Corn (in the husk)
3-4 Cups of Melted, Unsalted, Sweet Cream Butter
Salt and Pepper
Cayenne Pepper
Variety Seasonings, See Seasoned Butters, Page 14

Pull back the husk of each ear of Corn and remove silks. Holding the corn by the husks, rinse under running water. Cut off the last inch of the tip of the ear. Remove and discard some of the outer husks leaving a layer of three or four inner husks to completely enclose Corn. Tie husks in place with kitchen twin if needed. Soak Corn in sink or tub of water. Place Corn on hot charcoal grill to cook, using long handled tongs, turn frequently to insure even cooking. (Do not Butter or season corn while cooking). Cook until ears are steamed/cooked through and season by opening husks and dipping Corn in seasoned Butters and sprinkling with Salt and Pepper.

Fried Yams

What a wonderful, easy and tasty accompaniment. Try these with your next big celebration for a thoroughly delicious and unique treat to accompany your other celebration foods.

2-3 pounds of Sweet Potatoes (depending upon number of guests)

White Sugar

Butter as needed for number of pieces

Cinnamon

Thoroughly wash each yam and smooth the skins. Carefully microwave the desired number of yams until "medium-soft". Cool; then slice each to approximately ½" thick slices. Dip the slices in White Sugar and sauté in Butter on both sides until glazed. Drain on brown paper. Sprinkle with Cinnamon and serve warm.

Skillet Corn Bread

2 ½ cups Yellow corn Meal

1 cup flour

½ teaspoon Salt

4 teaspoons Baking Powder

3 Tablespoons Sugar

3 Eggs

2 cups Milk

½ cup Salad Oil

½ cup Cream Style Corn

10-12 slices crisp Fried Bacon (crumbled)

1 small jar chopped Pimento (drained)

1 ½ cups grated Cheddar Cheese (mild, medium
       or sharp)

1 large Onion, finely chopped

1 small can mild Green Chilies (drained)

Sift dry ingredients together. Add remaining ingredients and pour mixture into a hot, greased cast iron skillet. (To prepare skillet, pour ½ cup oil into skillet and place in preheated (400 degree) oven until oil smokes. Carefully pour out hot oil into a deep sink and immediately pour the corn bread mixture into the hot skillet. Place in preheated (400 degree) oven and bake for 45 minutes. Top of Corn Meal with be golden brown with a few darker brown areas . This is a large, thick recipe. Insure that inside of the bread is cooked through by inserting knife in center.   Use at least an 18 inch skillet.

MARKET LIST: Chicken (frying size), Fresh Corn in the husk, White and Green Onions, Corn Meal, Flour, Sugar, Eggs, Milk, Salad Oil, Various Seasonings, Green Chilies, Pimento, Bacon, Butter, Apple Cider Vinegar, Poke Sallet (or substitute greens), Vegetable Oil, Tea, Beer, Watermelons, Sweet Potatoes, Cinnamon, Grated Cheddar Cheese, Cream style Corn

JUNETEENTH CELEBRATION MENU #2
COOKOUT FOR LARGE GROUP

Crawfish Boil
Charcoal Turkey Legs
Charcoal Sausage Links
Okra Gumbo
Rustic Bread with Honey Butter
Corn Fritters
Beer and Iced Tea
Funnel Cakes
Pralines
Shaved Ice Cups

Just South of Houston, Texas, the beautiful George Ranch Historical Park, Richmond, Texas, hosts a variety of events and educational programs during the year. The charcoal/wood cooking techniques and many of the recipes in this section were obtained at the Juneteenth Celebration at the ranch a number of years back. The beautiful giant Oak Tree and observation deck which introduce this section, are located on this incredible property.

Crawfish Boil

60 pounds live Crawfish

Crawfish, Crab and Shrimp Boil Seasoning

12 – 15 Ears Sweet Corn, Husked, cleaned (silks removed)
and cut into 4 inch lengths

24 Red New Potatoes

Water to fill a 40 – 60 Quart Crawfish Pot

This is a favorite Cajun food and recipe adopted to accommodate the Juneteenth celebrations in parts of the South. Crawfish are available in most seafood markets and by fed-ex delivery from Gulf Coast commercial seafood suppliers who guarantee "live delivery". The typical "boil" is in a large 40, 60 quart cooker on a metal rack which is heated by a Propane burner, however, many celebrations include Crawfish Boils for hundreds. Crawfish must be cooked "live" and the seasonings are commercially available throughout the South. The water must be at a boil and Potatoes and Corn are to be started a few minutes before the Crawfish are placed in the pot. When done, the traditional "presentation" is to cover any picnic table or other flat surface with newspaper or white freezer wrap, scoop the cooked crawfish, potatoes and corn from the pot, spread over the newspaper, snap off the head of the Crawfish, open the tender shell, eat the crawfish and enjoy (often accompanied by a "cold beer"). Heads are reserved for "sucking" - a ritual enjoyed by many, shunned by others.

Charcoal Turkey Legs, Sausage Links

Turkey Legs and Sausage Links

The two most prominent meats prepared at most outdoor cookouts/celebrations celebrating Juneteenth are Turkey Legs (the large lower leg of the bird) and Sausage Links, commonly called "links". Turkey Legs are commercially available at meat markets and commercial suppliers and links are available at most supermarkets, however, the bulk suppliers are typically large meat markets and warehouse suppliers.

Turkey Legs are prepared on charcoal cookers, ordinarily the commercially branded charcoal is the foundation for the cooking /ire, but is frequently supplemented with hardwoods such as Mesquite and Hickory (usually chips), and other woods soaked in water to occasionally top off the charcoal in order to produce smoke to season the meat. Preparation must begin well in advance of the event, and the cooks at this event had arrived very early, started an early fire and began cooking 3 to 4 hours before the crowd arrived. Seasonings are usually a mix of salt, pepper, ground garlic, cayenne and onion powder. Liquid sauces are not used.

Links used for large "Bar B Que" events are typically a combination of Beef and Pork. There are many varieties available, however, and for personal consumption one might choose the gourmet varieties which offer a variety of specialty stuffing now including cheeses, chicken, duck and venison. Links cook quickly, however, the longer they are in the charcoal and wood smoke grill, the better the flavor. They are ordinarily moved off the direct/ire to a "holding spot" on the grill. There are no additional seasonings necessary to prepare links and like their "cook out partner", tomato and liquid sauces are never used. They are often served on a stick (to be eaten as the person is walking around) or in a bun with a variety of condiments.

Okra Gumbo
(to serve 100)

The Roux

2 cups Vegetable Oil

5 cups Flour

Make the Roux by heating Vegetable Oil in large pot over medium to high heat. Add Flour, stirring in about 2 cups at a time, allow to dissolve and continue to cook and stir until mixture turns a dark brown.

4 large White Onions	4 – 6 pounds of Okra
3 bunches Green Onions	5 large bags cleaned, headless,
4 stalks Celery	tailless Shrimp
4 Green Bell Peppers	4 – 6 pounds Crab Meat
6 cans Tomato Sauce with Tomato Bits	6 cloves Fresh Garlic
3 teaspoons Salt	2 teaspoons Cayenne Pepper
4 Tablespoons Gumbo File'	6 Bay Leaves

In advance of Roux preparation, clean and chop all vegetables and prepare Shrimp, Crab and Okra. (If using fresh Shrimp and Crab Meat, clean and store in refrigerator until needed and add the delicate crab meat last). Add Onions, Celery, Bell Peppers, Garlic, Salt, Cayenne Pepper, and stir into Roux. Add Tomato Sauce, Gumbo File' and Bay Leaves. Cook and stir vegetables to blend flavors and add water, one gallon at a time, stirring carefully. Bring to a boil, reduce heat and cook for 20 – 30 minutes. Remove Bay Leaves, add Gumbo File, Okra, Shrimp and cook slowly until flavors are blended and dish forms a thick soup, about 2 hours. Add Crab Meat for final hour of cooking. Taste and adjust Salt seasoning.

Rustic White Bread

2 cups warm Water, 110 degrees	3 teaspoons active dry Yeast
5 cups Bread Flour	2 teaspoons Sea Salt

Combine Yeast and water, let stand 5 minutes. In mixing bowl, combine flour, Salt and Yeast. Beat dough with mixer at medium speed. Knead dough 10-12 minutes until smooth dough forms. Place dough in large bowl, cover tightly with plastic wrap and let rise 1 to 2 hours. Remove and knead dough , shaping into a ball and transfer to a LaCloche baking dish if available, dust top with flour. Allow to rise a second time until doubled. Make 3 shallow Xs on top of loaf with a sharp knife and bake 1 hour until golden brown and sounds hollow when tapped on bottom.

Corn Fritters
(Foundation Recipe for Fritters)

2 Eggs

2/3 cup Milk

½ teaspoon Salt

1 teaspoon melted Butter

1 cup Flour

1 teaspoon Baking Powder

Beat Eggs slightly, add Milk, Salt and melted Butter. Add Flour, sifted with Baking Powder. Beat with electric mixer until smooth. May use immediately or store in covered bowl and keep in refrigerator for several days. Add variation desired and fry in deep hot fat (380 degrees) for 3 -5 minutes.

VARIATIONS: Cheese Fritters - Add ½ cup Grated American Cheese

Rice Fritters – Add 1 Tablespoon Sugar and 1 cup of Cooked Rice. Serve with Jelly

Vegetable Fritters – Add 1 cup of Corn or dip pieces of chopped Vegetables into
Batter, i.e., Cauliflower, Tomato, Broccoli, Onion, etc.

Fruit Fritters – Add 1 Tablespoon Sugar and mix. Dip slices of Apple, Pineapple or
other fruits into batter and fry.

Funnel Cakes

At events like Juneteenth celebrations, fairs, craft sales and art shows around the state, there are often vendors of Funnel Cakes. The fragrance of their sweet fried treats is enticing making them very popular for both children and adults. The cakes are made in small batches, fried, dusted with powdered Sugar and usually placed on paper plates or in small bags for the customer/guest. This recipe is universal and includes the following:

1-1/2 cups Flour   ¼ cup Sugar

2 teaspoons Baking Powder   ½ teaspoon Baking Soda

2 Eggs   Dash of Salt

1 cup Milk   1 cup Powdered Sugar

1 teaspoon Vanilla   2-3 Cups Vegetable Oil

Sift together Flour, Baking Powder, Baking Soda, Granulated Sugar and Salt in large bowl.

Beat Eggs, Milk and Vanilla together until blended. Combine with Flour mixture and mix well.

Heat Oil, drop small amount of mixture in oil. It is ready when mix comes to top immediately.

Prepare in batches, drizzling mixture into hot oil from large spoons full of batter, allowing strings of batter to form. Turn cake to brown both sides. Remove when cooked through and sprinkle both sides with Powdered Sugar. Serve immediately.

Pecan Pralines

These delicious "sweet treats" are enjoyed by both all nationalities, but are very popular with the Mexican and Black populations and are often found at festivals, Mexican restaurants, fast food stores and various other candy sales locations. Juneteenth vendors have a variety of sweets and treats, but these were my most appreciated. There are many recipes for Pecan Pralines, some use a mix or granulated and brown Sugars. This one has worked in testing.

2 cups Sugar

1 cup Buttermilk

1 teaspoon Soda

2-3 cups Pecan Halves

1/8th teaspoon Salt

2 Tablespoons Butter

½ teaspoon Vanilla

Combine Sugar, Soda, Buttermilk and Salt in heavy pot. Cook and stir until temperature reaches 210 degrees on candy thermometer. Add Butter, Vanilla, Pecans and continue cooking and stirring until candy comes to soft ball stage (235 degrees). Remove from heat and allow to cool slightly. Beat mixture until it becomes thick and creamy. Drop by tablespoons onto wax paper and cool.

SHAVED ICE CUPS

These refreshing treats are available from vendors (usually with just a cart with bottles of sweet syrups and a bin of shave/crushed ice). They are also popular in parts of Mexico and South Texas. To prepare this refreshing treat on a hot day in June, we need shaved (we will use crushed) ice and a sweet syrup made of your favorite juice (frozen Orange, Strawberry or Lemonade) work. Sweeten frozen juice with a combination of Sugar, Maple Syrup and Honey. Mix into frozen juices until thickened and adjust to taste. Pour over crushed ice in a plastic coated paper cup. Serve with spoon and straw.

MARKET LIST: Live Crawfish, Crawfish Seasoning, New Potatoes, Corn, Beer, Tea, Sausage Links, Turkey Legs, Bar b que seasonings, Charcoal, Hard Woods, White and Green Onions, Green Bell Peppers, Celery, Tomato Sauce with Tomato Bits, Okra, Shrimp, Crab Meat, Gumbo File', Bay Leaves, Garlic, Yeast, Bread Flour, Vegetable Oil, Eggs, Sugar, Milk Butter, Baking Powder, Baking Soda, Vanilla, Powdered Sugar, Grated American Cheese, Sea Salt, Honey, Frozen Fruit Juices, Crushed Ice, Buttermilk

FOURTH OF JULY
HOLIDAY COOKOUT MENU #1

Appetizers

Onion Dip, Bean Dip and Spinach Dip
Presented with Bread Sticks, Tortilla Chips and Vegetable Tray
(Celery Strips, Carrots, Cauliflower, Green Onions, Bell Pepper Strips)

Iced Tea with Lemons and Limes
Cold Beer, Chilled Sauvignon Blanc, Bloody Mary

Main Course

Beef Brisket Cooked on the Grill
Ginger Baked Beans
Zucchini Casserole
Mustard Green Beans and Cherry Tomatoes
French Bread Loaf with Garlic, Italian Seasoning, Butter
Australian Combined Merlot and Cabernet Sauvignon
Fruit Compote
Fresh Ground Coffee

Onion Dip

1 (16 ounce container Sour Cream)
1 package French Onion Soup Mix

Prepare the day before. Mix the Sour Cream and Soup Mix thoroughly, place in covered container, refrigerates.

Bean Dip

1 medium White Onion, Chopped
¼ cup Vegetable Oil
1 can Refried Beans
Dash of Sea Salt

1 seeded, chopped Jalapeno (if desired)
Dash of Tabasco Sauce (f desired)
1 ½ cup Grated Cheddar Cheese

Sauté Onion in Vegetable Oil until clarified and beginning to brown. Add Refried Beans and Mix well. Add Grated Cheddar Cheese and continue to stir and incorporate cheese into mix. Add a dash of Sea Salt and either chopped Jalapeno or Tabasco if desired. Stir and serve with Tortilla Chips

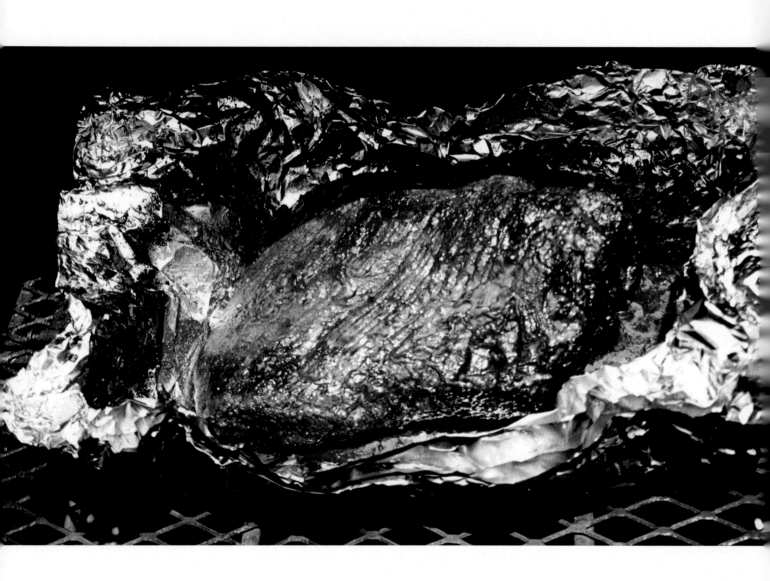

Spinach Dip

1 Box frozen Chopped Spinach

1 8 oz container Sour Cream

4-6 Green Onions (tips only)

½ cup chopped Fresh Parsley

Tablespoon fresh squeezed Lemon Juice

2 Tablespoons Miracle Whip

Thaw and drain Spinach, press in colander to remove all water. Chop Green Onions and Parsley and combine with Sour Cream and Spinach. Stir in Miracle Whip and Lemon Juice. Place in air tight container, chill and serve cold.

Serve the various Dips above on a large tray with an assortment of fresh vegetables, bread sticks and chips.

Beef Brisket Cooked on the Grill

The preparation of a tender Brisket begins in the selection and purchasing stage. Select a Brisket which has not been trimmed. My experience is that the most desirable meat of this type is one which is prepared with all the marbling intact as presented by the butcher. I do not remove any fat from the Brisket bought from the butcher. However, there are som preparation techniques which will ensure a tender desirable product. Begin preparations the day before serving – Always. Briskets have to be marinated and tenderized to produce a flavorful and tender result. There are a number of marinades available in commercial form or you may take your own. Among the choices I prefer are Cajun Injector Marinade for beef, pork and wild game used also as a tenderizing marinade, followed by a rubdown with Zach's Original Bar-B-Que seasonings prior to cooking.

Commercial unseasoned meat tenderizer is also recommended. Use sparingly. Always begin by slowly cooking your brisket in a covered or aluminum foil wrap for at least 2 hours on a charcoal grill set back from the heat. Then open aluminum foil covering and bring brisket closer to the heat of the charcoal or wood burning grill and continue to cook/smoke for another 2 to 3 hours until the meat is cooked through and tender. Turn the brisket several times during the cooking process to allow meat to absorb cooking/smoking flavors. Always slice using a diagonal cut crossways of the grain. You get a better flavor if you are using a charcoal or wood smoke. You can cook a brisket up to 8 to 10 hours and cold-smoke longer for added flavor. Do not boil a brisket or oven-bake in water as some recipes recommend.

Ginger Baked Beans

1 pound dried Navy Beans

2 teaspoons prepared Dijon Mustard

1 small white Onion

Picked over and rinsed

½ cup Tomato Sauce

1/3 cup Unsulphured Molasses

2 Tablespoons Dark Brown Sugar

2 Tablespoons Maple Syrup

1 ½ teaspoons Ground Ginger

2 whole Cloves

2 ounces Salt Pork (in once piece,

rinsed and dried

Soak the beans in water to cover for 6 to 8 hours. Preheat oven to 400 degrees. Drain the Beans and place in a 2 ½ quart glazed bean pot or covered casserole.

In a small saucepan, combine the Tomato Sauce, Molasses, Sugar, Maple Syrup, Mustard and Ginger. Bring to a simmer and cook, stirring for about four minutes, or until the Sugar is dissolved. Pour the mixture over the beans. Add 2 cups of water and stir to blend.

Cut the Onion in half lengthwise, stopping just above the roots so the halves remain attached. Turn the Onion 90 degrees and repeat. Stick the Cloves into the Onion. Add the Onion to the bean pot (it will float). With a sharp knife, score the skin of the Salt Pork, making 2 to 3 cuts diagonally in each direction. Place the Salt Pork, fat side down, in the bean pot.

Bake for 1 hour. Reduce the temperature to 250 degrees and continue baking for 5 to 6 hours, until the Beans are soft.

Mustard Green Beans and Cherry Tomatoes

1 ½ pounds Green Beans, trimmed and cut

    Into 1 inch pieces

3 Tablespoons Balsamic Vinegar

2 teaspoons Sugar

1 teaspoon Salt

¼ cup finely chopped Red Onion

1 pint Cherry Tomatoes, halved

Freshly ground Black Pepper

2 teaspoons Dijon Mustard

¼ cup Olive Oil

In a large pot of boiling salted water, cook the Beans until just crisp-tender, about 3 minutes. Drain and place in a serving bowl.In medium bowl, whisk together Vinegar, Sugar, Mustard, Salt and Oil. Stir in Red Onion. Drizzle dressing over warm Beans; top Beans with Tomatoes and sprinkle Black Pepper over all. Serve warm or at room temperature. Serves eight.

MARKET LIST: Sour Cream, Green and White Onions, Red Onion, Cherry Tomatoes, Dijon Mustard, Green Beans, Balsamic Vinegar, Sugar, Vegetable Oil, Jalapenos, Tabasco Sauce, Canned Refried Beans, grated Cheddar Cheese, Tortilla Chips, Cauliflower, Bread Sticks, Bell Peppers, Lemons and Limes, Beer, Sauvignon Blanc, Bloody Mary Mix, Gin, Celery, Zucchini Squash, Italian Bread crumbs, French Onion soup Mix, Beef Brisket, Chopped Spinach, frozen, Fresh Parsley, Miracle Whip, Charcoal, Dried Navy Beans, Tomato Sauce, Molasses, Brown Sugar, Maple Syrup, Whole Cloves, Salt Pork, Ground Ginger, Olive Oil, grated Mozzarella Cheese, Italian Sausage, Butter, Blackberries, Strawberries, Whipping Cream, Vanilla

Zucchini Casserole

2-1/2 pounds Zucchini Squash

1 large White Onion

½ small White Onion (chopped fine)

1 ½ - 2 cups Italian Style Bread Crumbs

2 Tablespoons Olive Oil

2 Eggs

1 twelve ounce package Grated
   Mozarella Cheese

1 16 ounce package Italian Sausage (mild)

Italian Seasoning

4 Tablespoons Butter

Salt and Pepper

Cut off ends of Zucchini and cut in ½ inch slices. Do not peel. Chop large Onion and combine with Squash in boiling water. Add Olive Oil and Salt and Pepper. Sauté Sausage and small onion. Cool and drain well.

When Zucchini is just tender, remove from heat, and drain in large metal colander. Return to pan, add Bread Crumbs and Italian seasonings and toss to combine. Lightly beat eggs and add, stirring gently. Season to taste.

Place one layer of Zucchini Squash (one half of mixture) in bottom of Buttered casserole dish and top with Sausage and Onion (reserving one half cup). Layer half of Mozarella Cheese over the Sausage, and then place remaining Zucchini over Sausage. Cover with remaining Mozarella and crumble the reserved Sausage on top.

Bake at 350 degrees for 35 -40 minutes until done and Cheese is browned.

Fruit Compote

FILLING

1 large box Blackberries

1 large box Strawberries

1 large box Raspberries

(Add any seasonal fresh fruit desired)

Whipping Cream

1 cup Sugar

1 Tablespoon Vanilla

Wash berries, drain in colander. Whip cream with Vanilla and Sugar (to taste). Fold into berries and put into individual Pastry Shells.

SHELLS

2 cups Sifted Flour

1 teaspoon Salt

¾ cup Solid Vegetable Shortening

4 Tablespoons water

Mix Flour and Salt, cut in Vegetable Shortening with pastry blender until mixture is very fine. Add water, a Tablespoon at a time and blend. Roll into a ball and refrigerate for 2 hours. Remove from refrigerator, roll on a floured flat surface and cut into rounds. Place in individual tart shells and bake until lightly brown and crisp. Fill with Fruit mixture. Chill

FOURTH OF JULY SUMMER MENU #2

Appetizer

Buffalo Wings
Wine Coolers

Main Course

Fried Whole Catfish with Lemon and Lime Slices
Hush Puppies
Green Pepper Cole Slaw
Home Fries
Raspberry and Mint Tea

Dessert

Apple Pie w/Vanilla Ice Cream

Buffalo Wings

2 pounds Chicken Wings

Cut between joint and remove wing tips

1 Tablespoon Garlic Salt

1 Tablespoon Cayenne Pepper

(for less spicy wings, reduce Cayenne Pepper)

2 teaspoons Ground Ginger

¼ cup Sesame Oil

1 Cup Buffalo Barbecue Sauce

Wings are marinated in a plastic bag containing Sesame Oil, Garlic Salt, Cayenne Pepper, Ginger. Coat all wings in mixture and marinate until grill has reached white coal stage. Place chicken on direct heat, turn frequently and cook until wings are cooked through. Baste with Barbecue Sauce during last 10 – 15 minutes turning and basting over grill to uniformly cover wings with sauce. Serve wings with a Blue Cheese salad dressing.

Wine Coolers:

For refreshing Summertime coolers, mix Chablis with your choice of Lime and Lemon Juice and shake or stir in frozen Pineapple or Grapefruit Juice. Shake and serve over ice.

Mix a Zinfandel with Strawberry Soda and top with fresh Strawberries, serve over ice.

Mix Chablis with Lemon/Lime Soda, serve over crushed ice.

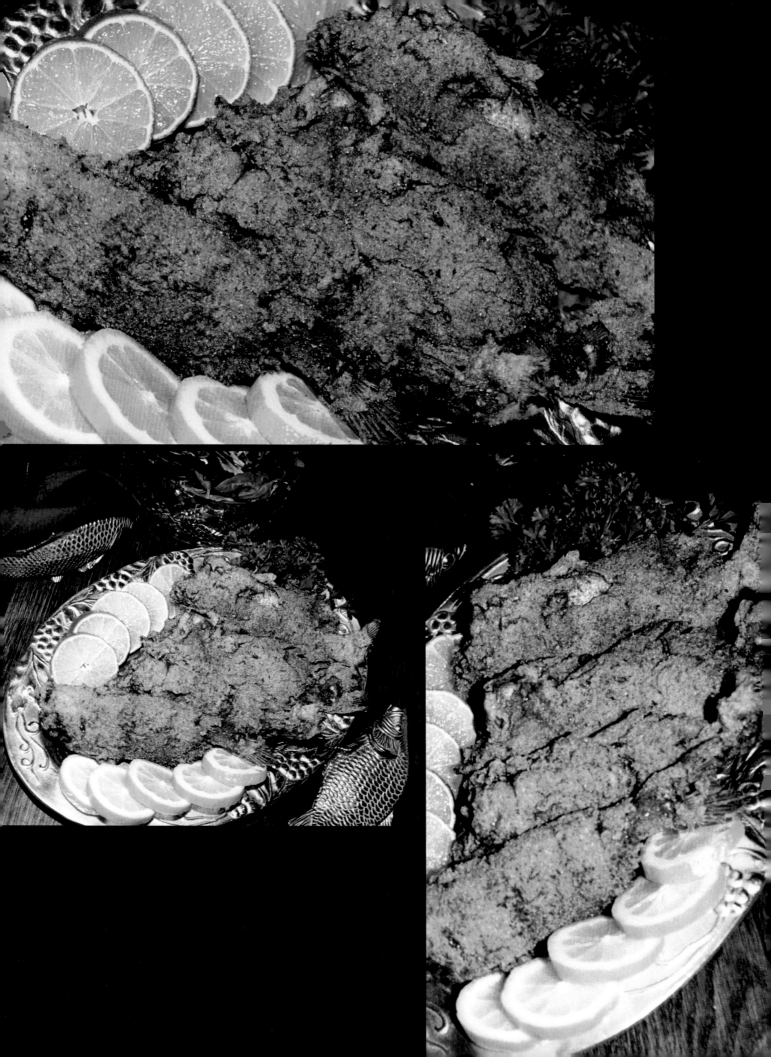

Fried Whole Catfish

4 cleaned Catfish, heads removed

Approximately ¼ pound each

2 cups Yellow Corn Meal

¾ cup Flour

2 teaspoons Salt

2-3 teaspoons fine grind Black Pepper

1 teaspoon Paprika

2 Eggs

1 cup Milk

¼ to ½ gallon Vegetable Oil or

   Peanut Oil (amount needed to completely

      cover Fish while frying)

Rinse Catfish and place in ice water while preparing batter. Keep fish wet and do not drain or damp dry. Beat Eggs and add Milk. Place Corn Meal, Flour, Salt, Pepper and Paprika in large flat dish or on large sheet of aluminum foil and mix well.

Heat Oil to 350 degrees. Lift Catfish from ice water, roll in Corn Meal mixture, dip in Milk mixture, then roll again in Corn Meal mixture. Immediately place Fish in heated oil using tongs. Cook until golden brown and cooked through – 15 to 20 minutes.

Note: Larger fish will require longer cooking time. Increase the Corn Meal and Milk mixture proportionately if preparing larger number of whole fried Catfish or using larger fish.

Serve with your favorite Seafood Sauce, sliced Lemons and Limes and Tartar Sauce.

Hush Puppies

2 cups Cornmeal

4 Tablespoons Baking Powder

1 cup Flour

2 Eggs, beaten

¾ cup Milk (more if needed)

1 Tablespoon Oil

Salt, Red Pepper and Black Pepper, to taste

4 cups Vegetable Oil for Frying

1 diced Jalapeno

1 Green Bell Pepper, diced

1 large White Onion, chopped fine

4 -6 pods of fresh Garlic, chopped

Mix together Cornmeal, Baking Powder, Flour and add Eggs, Milk and 1 Tablespoon Oil.

Mix well and stir in diced Jalapeno, Bell pepper, Onion and Garlic. Season with Red Pepper flakes and Black Pepper. Roll into "golf ball" sized rolls .

Heat Vegetable Oil in a deep fryer and fry Hush Puppies until golden brown and cooked through. Remove from oil with slotted spoon and drain on paper towels. Serve hot with fish.

Green Pepper Cole Slaw

4 cups Green Cabbage, shredded

1 cup Red Cabbage, chopped

½ cup Green Bell Pepper, chopped

1 cup Yellow Bell Pepper, chopped

2 Tablespoons Sugar

Coarse Ground Black Pepper

2 Tablespoons Tarragon Vinegar

½ cup Italian Salad Dressing

1 teaspoon prepared Mustard

4 Green Onions, chopped

1 teaspoon Salt

1 teaspoon Celery Seed

In large mixing bowl, combine shredded red and green Cabbage, chopped Green and Yellow Bell Peppers, Chopped Green Onions and mix thoroughly.

In separate bowl combine Sugar, Salt and Pepper, Celery Seed and add Vinegar, Salad Dressing and Mustard. Mix well and pour over vegetables. Toss until Cabbage mixture is well covered and place in refrigerator until ready to serve. Serve on large Purple Cabbage Leaves.

Home Fries

6 Medium Idaho Potatoes

1 Medium White Onion

Vegetable Oil for frying

Sea Salt/coarse ground Black Pepper

Peel and slice Potatoes in ¼ inch slices. Peel and slice Onion in ¼ to ½ inch slices and mix with Potatoes. Heat Oil in large cast iron skillet over medium heat. Add Potatoes and Onions and fry until golden brown. Turn and repeat. Turn cooked, brown Potatoes and Onions on heated platter and Salt and Pepper to Taste.

MARKET LIST: Chicken Wings, Chablis and Zinfandel Wines, Cayenne Pepper, Ground Ginger, Sesame Oil, Barbecue Sauce, Cayenne Pepper, Whole Catfish, Vegetable Oil, Corn Meal, Milk, Eggs, Flour, Paprika, Jalapenos, Green and White Onions, Yellow and Green Bell Pepper, Baking Powder, Fresh Garlic, Red Pepper, Purple and Green Cabbage, Vegetable Oil, Apples, Potatoes, Vanilla Ice Cream, Lemon and Lime Soda, Frozen Juices, Strawberry and Pineapple, fresh Strawberries

Halloween Treats (No Tricks)

There are few traditional "meals" associated with celebrating Halloween. The typical "trick or treat" items are candies given out to neighborhood children who dress in their finest scariest outfit and ordinarily arrive in groups of 5 to 15 expressing their demands for treats or you will be "tricked". The holiday has become a very popular occasion for American children. Traditionally, however, Candied Popcorn Balls, Pumpkin Pie and Brandied Drinks are an indication that the fall season has arrived and that winter is approaching. In celebration, the following recipes are included here for memory sake and to warm your heart and hearth.

Popcorn Balls

Caramel Peanuts and Popcorn Balls   1 stick Butter
8 cups freshly popped Popcorn   ½ cup Corn Syrup
1 package of roasted and salted Peanuts   1 teaspoon Vanilla
1 cup packed Brown Sugar
½ teaspoon Baking Soda

Place popped Corn and Peanuts in baking dish in a warm oven, 250 – 300 degrees. Mix Brown Sugar, Butter, Corn Syrup together in a medium saucepan and bring mixture to a boil. Continue to boil until Syrup reaches soft ball stage. Remove from heat and add Vanilla and Baking Soda. Mix sauce in Popcorn and Peanuts and bake mixture until Caramel is thoroughly incorporated into the Popcorn, approximately an hour. Mix frequently with a spatula.

Marshmallow Popcorn Balls
10 cups freshly popped, unsalted Popcorn (place in large mixing bowl)
3 cups Miniature Marshmallows
1 ½ sticks Sweet Cream Butter
3 – 4 Tablespoons Gelatin, Cherry or Raspberry

Melt Butter and Marshmallows in medium saucepan. Stir in Gelatin and mix well.

Apple Pie with Vanilla Ice Cream

As American as Apple Pie – this is one of the most enjoyed and "old custom" desserts made in this country. For Apple Pie, it is important to use baking apples – the Pippin and Granny Smith are good choices, although there are several other varieties which are good "cooking quality". This dish is often served warm with Cheddar Cheese Slices and I encourage that service during the colder months. It is also perfectly acceptable to vary the seasonings in this dish to include Vanilla, Nutmeg and Brown Sugar. Experiment and enjoy.

FOR THE CRUST

2 cups sifted enriched Flour

1 teaspoon Salt

¾ cup Solid Shortening

4 Tablespoons cold water

Mix all ingredients together, divide and form into two balls, refrigerate for one hour.

Remove from refrigerator, place on floured surface, and roll into round disc shape to fit 9" pie pan. Place crust in pie plate and allow to hang over sides – do not trim. Pierce several openings in the bottom shell.

FOR THE FILLING

3 Tablespoons all purpose Flour

1 cup Sugar

1 ½ teaspoons Cinnamon

6 Large Cooking Apples, Granny Smith or Pippin
    Peeled, cored and sliced

¼ cup melted Butter

Combine Sugar, Cinnamon, Flour and melted Butter. Sprinkle over Apples and toss to cover. Place Apples in prepared crust. Roll out second pastry ball to cover 9" pie plate dimensions. Fold in half and make several cuts in top crust. Place over pie filling, align edges of both crusts, crimp edges of pie crusts. Sprinkle Sugar over top crust and bake in preheated oven at 350 degrees until crust is golden brown and Apples are cooked.

Serve pie with preferred brand Vanilla Ice Cream.

Brandied Pumpkin Pie with Crispy Pie Crust

CRUST

1 ½ cups Flour (sifted)

½ teaspoon Salt

½ cup Crisco Solid Shortening

3 Tablespoons water

Combine Flour, Salt and Shortening. Cut Shortening in with pastry blender until mix is free of large shortening pieces. Add chilled water to flour mix and mix. Avoid over mixing.

Refrigerate for an hour or two if possible. Remove from refrigerator and roll out on floured surface about 14 -15 inches. Place in lightly floured 9" or 10" pie pan. Fold under and crimp sides of Crust and prick bottom of crust with fork.

FILLING

1 16 ounce can Pumpkin	½ teaspoon ground Cloves
2/3 cup packed Brown Sugar	2 Eggs, slightly beaten
½ teaspoon Salt	1 13 oz can Evaporated Milk
1 teaspoon ground Cinnamon	¼ cup Brandy
½ teaspoon ground Ginger	1 Unbaked 9 inch Pie Shell
¼ teaspoon ground Nutmeg	Whipping Cream and 2 Tbsp Chilled Brandy

In a large bowl, combine pumpkin, Brown Sugar, Salt and Spices. Blend in Eggs, Evaporated Milk, and the ¼ cup Brandy. Pour into pastry shell. Bake in 400 degree oven for 45 minutes or till knife inserted halfway between center and edge comes out clean. Just before serving, prepare whipped cream topping, beating until stiff peaks form. Add chilled Brandy and continue beating to maintain form. Cut wedges of pie and serve with a dollop of brandied cream. Serve pie with cups of hot coffee.

Aunt Nelda's Peanut Brittle

2 cups Sugar	½ cup Water
2 cups raw, shelled Peanuts	2 teaspoons Baking Soda
1 cup light Corn Syrup	2 Tablespoons Butter
1 teaspoon Vanilla	

Prepare two Buttered Cookie Sheets.

Combine Sugar, Corn Syrup and Water in medium sauce pan. Cook and stir until mixture reaches soft ball stage (230 degrees). Add Butter and shelled Peanuts and continue to cook, stirring continuously until mixture reaches hard crack stage (300 degrees). Remove from heat and stir in Vanilla and Baking Soda. Mixture will fizz, stir down quickly and mix well. Quickly spread half the mixture onto one sheet and smooth with spatula or back of spoon and move quickly to spread the remaining candy on to the second cookie sheet.

Pumpkin Cheesecake

1 ½ cups Graham Cracker Crumbs

3 Tablespoons plus 1 cup (8 oz) Sugar

1 teaspoon ground Ginger

6 Tablespoons unsalted Butter, melted

1 ½ lb Cream Cheese at room temperature

1 ¾ cups (1 pound) Pumpkin Puree, at room temperature

1 teaspoon finely grated Orange Zest

1 Tablespoon Ground Cinnamon

½ teaspoon Ground Cloves

½ teaspoon Ground Nutmeg

6 Eggs, lightly beaten

Preheat the oven to 325 degrees. Position rack in middle of oven. Cover outside and bottom of a 9 inch springform pan with heavy-duty aluminum foil, shiney side out. Butter the inside of the pan and set aside.

THE CRUST

Stir together the Cracker Crumbs, 3 Tablespoons Sugar and the Ginger. Gradually add melted Butter and stir and toss until well mixed. Press the mixture evenly over the inside of the springform pan and press 1 ¾ to 2 inches up the sides of the pan. Chill.

THE CHEESECAKE

Place the Cream Cheese in a large bowl. Beat with electric mixer until light and fluffy – 2 -3 minutes. Slowly add the cup of Sugar beating continuously. Scrape down sides of bowl. Add the Pumpkin, Orange Zest, Cinnamon, Cloves and Nutmeg and beat mixture until smooth. Add eggs, 1/3 of the mixture at a time, beating well after each addition and scraping down sides of bowl. Stir with spatula to dispel any bubbles.

Pour the batter into the prepared pan. Bake until the top is lightly puffed all over – 60 – 70 minutes. The center may be slightly underset; it will firm up during cooling. Cool on a wire rack, then remove the foil and pan sides and refrigerate overnight. Serve on a large flat serving plate decorated with candied fruit if desired. Slice Cheesecake chilled.

THANKSGIVING DINNER MENU #1

Appetizer

Forum Famous Cheese Ring
Champagne or Sparkling Wine

Main Course

Roast Turkey
Cornbread Dressing
Giblet Gravy
Orange Stuffed Cranberry Sauce
Broccoli with Lemon Sauce
Sweet Potatoes with Pecan, Marshmallow Dressing
Layered fresh Spinach Salad
All Bran Refrigerator Rolls

Dessert

Brandy Alexander Cheesecake
Fresh Ground Hot Coffee

Forum Famous Cheese Ring

1 pound Cheddar Cheese, grated
1 medium White Onion, grated
¾ cup Mayonnaise
1 cup chopped Pecans

1 Garlic clove, minced
½ teaspoon Hot Red Pepper Sauce
Raspberry or Strawberry Preserves

Combine Cheese, Onion, Mayonnaise, Pecans, Garlic and Pepper Sauce in large bowl and mix well. Place mixture in a 2 cup ring mold lined with plastic wrap.Chill in refrigerator overnight. Unmold and fill center with preserves. Serve with crisp toasted breads or crackers.

Broccoli with Lemon Sauce

1 bunch fresh Broccoli -1 ½ - 2 pounds
6 cups boiling water
Salt

¼ cup Olive Oil
1 clove Garlic, chopped fine
2 Tablespoons Lemon Juice

Remove large leaves and tough stems of Broccoli. Wash thoroughly, drain. Separate flowers splitting larger stalks into quarters. Place in a 6 quart saucepan. Add boiling water and 1 teaspoon Salt. Cook covered for ten minutes or until Broccoli is tender, drain in colander. Place Olive Oil and Garlic in pan, heat. Add Broccoli, sprinkle with Lemon Juice and ½ teaspoon Salt. Cook until Broccoli is heated through. Serve hot.

Roast Turkey and Cornbread Dressing

Thaw the Turkey overnight in the refrigerator. Remove Neck and Giblets from inside the bird and rinse in colander. Place in large pot of water, add 1 teaspoon salt , ½ teaspoon ground Black Pepper, 1 teaspoon Sage, four large cans Chicken Stock, and bring to a boil. Reduce heat and cook until giblets are tender and neck meat can be easily removed from bone. Reserve liquid.

Rinse bird in large sink insuring that cavities are clean. Pat dry with paper towels and refrigerate until ready to stuff.

1 double recipe Corn Bread

1 loaf thin sliced white Bread – day or two days old – toast about half the slices and break toasted and untoasted slices into 2 and 3 inch chunks into largest mixing bowl. Add:

1 large White Onion, chopped medium

1 bunch Green Onions, tips only, chopped

1 bunch Celery – outside canes stripped, chopped medium

4 large Eggs, whisked until just blended

2 sticks Butter, melted (do not use Margarine)

Salt, Black Pepper, Rubbed Sage

Corn Bread

NOTE: Always prepare Cornbread in a Cast Iron Skillet. You will need at least an 18" skillet.

2 cups Yellow Corn Meal	2/3 cup Flour	1 1/3 cup Milk
4 teaspoons Baking Powder	2 Eggs Beaten	
1 teaspoon Salt	¼ cup Vegetable Oil	

Mix all ingredients in the order given. Place ¼ cup Vegetable Oil in cast iron skillet and heat oil in preheated oven (450 degrees) until it begins to smoke. Carefully remove skillet from oven and pour Corn Bread mixture into pan. Return skillet to oven, bake until corn bread is golden brown and springs back to touch, about 25 30 minutes. Remove skillet and turn bread out on cutting block. When cooled, break into pieces and add to mixing bowl.

When Giblets and Neck are cooked tender, remove from the pot, cool and chop Gizzard and Liver. Strip neck meat from the bone and chop. Add all meats to the large mixing bowl and stir into bread.

Bring liquid to a boil, reduce heat and add sufficient liquid to bread mix to moisten all ingredients. Stir well to incorporate seasonings, adjust to taste. Stuff neck and large cavity of bird and place remaining stuffing in covered casserole and bake until cooked through. Uncover to brown during last 20 minutes. Roast stuffed Turkey according to required time for size/pounds of bird. Test doneness using meat thermometer in thickest part of breast. Thermometer should register 180-185 degrees. Baste frequently. Use Aluminum Foil tent to prevent over-browning.

Giblet Gravy

Note: If you plan to use the Giblets from your turkey in the stuffing, you may wish to purchase the packaged frozen giblets to make your Gravy. A rich brown gravy can be made to accompany the Turkey and Dressing for those who do not wish to use the Giblets in their stuffing or gravy preparations.

½ cup Vegetable Oil

½ cup Flour

1 cup whole Milk

1 ½ (more if needed) cup reserved liquid from
    Chicken Stock and Water, mixed

Salt and Pepper to taste

Brown flour in vegetable oil in skillet. Do not take the mixture to a roux. When browned, add cooked giblets, 2 Tablespoons of uncooked dressing mix, and water mixed with the chicken stock to thin the Gravy. Lower heat, add Salt and Pepper, cook and stir until all ingredients are heated through and gravy has reached the desired consistency. Add liquid as needed and stir well. This will produce a "brown gravy". For cream gravy, do not brown the Flour. Combine all ingredients and heat, add liquids to achieve desired consistency.

Oranges Stuffed with Homemade Cranberry Sauce

Prepare Cranberry Sauce from whole berries according to package directions. Chill .

Select 6 large Oranges, cut oranges at right and left angles (approximately one inch length cuts) completely around Orange to separate halves. Remove inside of Oranges and fill with Cranberry Sauce. Surround Roast Turkey with stuffed Oranges on large platter.

Layered Spinach Salad

Large package of Baby Spinach Leaves

2 Eight ounce containers Cream Cheese, Original

1 Eight ounce package Grated

1 small jar Miracle Whip

1 package frozen (baby) Green Peas

1 box sliced mushroom

1 bunch Green Onions

Mozzarella Cheese

1 Pound thin sliced Bacon

Rinse and dry Spinach leaves on paper towels. Remove any long stems. Combine Cream Cheese (softened) with Miracle Whip. Combine using electric mixer. Thaw and drain the frozen Green Peas. Chop Green Onions, use green tips only. Fry Bacon crisp and crumble when cooled. Beginning with the Spinach, layer the ingredients in a large glass (see through) bowl. Layers will be Spinach, Cream Cheese and Miracle Whip (combined), Green Peas, Sliced Mushrooms, Grated Mozzarella Cheese, Green Onions and Crushed Bacon.

All Bran Refrigerator Rolls

1 cup Solid Shortening

2/3 to ¾ cup Sugar

1 cup All-Bran Cereal

1 ½ to 3 teaspoons Salt

1 cup boiling Water

2 Eggs, well beaten

2 cakes or packages Yeast

1 cup lukewarm Water

6-6 ½ cups Flour

Combine Shortening, Sugar, Bran and Salt. Add boiling water. Stir until shortening is melted. Cool, add Eggs and Yeast which has been softened in lukewarm Water. Add 3 cups Flour and beat well. Add remaining Flour, beat well. Knead on flour cloth or board. Place in greased bowl. Cover. Let rise about one hour. Roll out onto floured surface, cut into desired shape, place in greased baking dish and allow to rise another 45 minutes to 1 hour. Bake in a 350- 375 degree oven for 20 minutes or until brown and cooked through. Serve with Sweet Cream Butter.

This mixture can hold for 3-4 days in the refrigerator in a sealed plastic bag. To bake, remove from refrigerator, place in greased bowl for 1 ½ to 2 hours, roll out in desired shape and allow to rise a second time for 45 minutes to 1 hour. Follow previous baking directions.

Brandy Alexander Cheesecake

CRUST

18 Chocolate Graham Cracker Boards

1 Tablespoon Sugar

½ cup (1 stick) Unsalted Butter, melted

In food processor, pulse Graham Crackers until fine crumbs are formed. Add Sugar and Butter, pulse until crumbs are moistened. Press into bottom and up side of a 9 inch springform pan. Refrigerate.

FILLING

4 packages (8 ounces each) Cream Cheese (softened)	4 Eggs
1 ¼ cups Sugar	3 Tablespoons Brandy
3 Tablespoons Cornstarch	3 Tablespoons Crème de Cacao

In a large bowl, beat Cream Cheese until smooth, about 1 minute. Add Sugar and Cornstarch, beat on medium-high speed until creamy, about 3 minutes. Add Eggs, one at a time - beating well after each addition. Add Brandy and Crème de Cacao, beat until smooth. Pour filling into crust.

Bake at 325 degrees until edge of Cheesecake is just set and center slightly jiggles (60 – 70 minutes). Transfer to wire rack. Run a thin knife around edge of pan. Let cool completely. Cover and refrigerate overnight.

GARNISH: Remove side of pan. Whip Heavy Cream and Sugar to stiff peaks. Drop dollops of Whipped Cream on top of Cheesecake. Scatter Toffee bits or Chocolate Chips on top of cream.

THANKSGIVING DINNER MENU #2

Appetizer

Fruit and Cheese Tray
Featuring Camembert, Gouda, Stilton Cheeses
Fruit and Vegetables peeled and sectioned
Presented on large serving platter on Leaf Lettuce
Pears, Apples, Orange Sections, Seedless Grapes,
Olives, Sweet Peppers, Bread Sticks, Variety Crackers

Main Course

Stuffed/Rolled Whole Filet Mignon
Horseradish Scalloped Potatoes
Mushroom, Squash and Bell Pepper Grill
Steamed Green Beans with Butter Sauce
Jim's Rolls
Butter
Hearty Red Australian Wine

Dessert

Bread Pudding
Brandy Alexander

Appetizer Fruit Tray

Purchase Block Cheeses and present with assorted Fruits, cored, sliced and peeled, as appropriate. Insure that extra long toothpicks are available and cheese shavers or knives as needed. Other Cheeses may be substituted, including some of the "soft cheeses" which can be spread on fruits such as pears and apples. This makes a striking presentation. Prepare sufficient back-up fruits and cheeses to refill as needed.

Stuffed Rolled Whole Filet Mignon

1 Whole Beef Filet Mignon

Box Mushrooms, sliced

Large Package Sun Dried Tomatoes

Large Purple Onion

Olive Oil

1 bunch Fresh Parsley

½ pound Romano Cheese, grated

1 large White Onion, Sliced thin

1 stick Sweet Cream Butter

1 bottle Red Table Wine

Have butcher remove any muscle or connective tissue from beef and Cut filet slightly more than halfway through. Sauté Mushrooms, Sun Dried Tomatoes, Purple Onion in Olive Oil until flavors is blended. Combine with Chopped Parsley and Romano Cheese. Mix well and spread the length of the inside of the filet. Fold and tie in several places with kitchen twine. Sauté White Onion and spread over top of Roast. Roast at 325 degrees until cooked rare.

Horseradish Scalloped Potatoes

This heavenly Gratin makes a creamy accompaniment to beef. If using prepared Horseradish, drain it well before adding.

3 ½ cups Heavy Cream

2 cloves Garlic, minced

1 ¾ teaspoons Salt

½ teaspoon fresh ground black pepper

6 Tablespoons Grated, peeled fresh

5-6 Idaho Potatoes, peeled and sliced thin

½ large Granny Smith Apple, peeled, halved,
    cored and thinly sliced

¼ cup Parmesan Cheese

Horseradish Root

Combine heavy Cream, Garlic, Salt and Pepper and Horseradish. Taste to determine amount of horseradish needed. Layer Potatoes and Apple in a 13 X 9 baking dish. Pour the Horseradish mix over the Potatoes. Bake at 350 degrees until bubbling, about 30 minutes. Sprinkle the Parmesan Cheese over the top and bake for 15 minutes longer, until Potatoes are tender and top is browned. Cover the Gratin with aluminum foil and keep in a warm place for 20 – 30 minutes before serving. Cut the Gratin in squares and serve.

Mushroom, Squash, Onion and Bell Pepper Grill

1 Pound Large Mushrooms

4 - 6 Zucchini Squash, Sliced in ½ inch slices

4 - 6 Yellow Squash, Sliced in ½ inch slices

1 Red, Yellow and Green Bell Pepper, Cleaned and
    Cut into 2 inch Slices

1 large Red Onion, Peeled and cut into 1 inch slices

1 Bottle Italian Dressing

½ cup Balsamic Vinegar or Red
Wine Vinegar

1 bunch fresh Thyme

1 bunch fresh Cilantro

3 – 4 cloves Garlic, chopped

Chop Herbs and Garlic and combine in bowl with Italian Dressing and Wine Vinegar. Beat to combine. Prepare Grill and insure that grate will not allow vegetables to fall through openings. Place vegetables on medium hot fire, brush and drizzle marinade on all vegetables and turn to cook through. Serve on warm platter with any unused marinade.

MARKET LIST: Cheeses (Camembert, Gouda, Stilton) Leaf Lettuce, Apples, Pears, Oranges, Sweet Peppers, Olives, Bread Sticks, Seedless Grapes, Butter, Australian Wine, Bread, Mushrooms, Sun Dried Tomatoes, Purple Onions, Grated Romano Cheese, Parsley, Red Table Wine, White and Green Onions, Brandy, Cream, Whole Filet Mignon Roast, Potatoes, Squash, Yellow, Red and Green Bell Peppers, Olive Oil, Zucchini Squash, Balsamic or Red Wine Vinegar, Italian Dressing, Fresh Garlic, Green Beans, Sea Salt, Yeast, Sugar, Shortening, Chopped Pecans, Raisins, Cinnamon, Nutmeg, Vanilla, French Bread Loaf, Canadian Whiskey, Cornstarch

Steamed Green Beans with Butter Sauce

Select Fresh Green Beans if available in your Supermarket. Snap ends and leave whole. Prepare Steamer with hot salted water and place cleaned beans in a steamer rack. Heat water to boiling, then reduce heat and cook for 10-15 minutes until beans are just tender. Test to be insure beans are cooked through.(Do not overcook). Place in warm serving bowl with lid. Melt two sticks Sweet Cream Butter and pour over Beans. Sprinkle with Sea Salt and freshly ground Black Pepper Corns.

Jim's Rolls

This simple recipe is another of those "treasures" in my favorite recipe file for more years than we are going to explore. It is a simple, never fail, recipe I hope you will enjoy adding to your "really easy recipe" list to use when you like. They are delicious

1 cake Yeast

¼ cup Lukewarm Water

1 teaspoon Sugar

Mix together.

Meanwhile, melt 4 Tablespoons Shortening

Add 1 teaspoon Salt

¼ cup Sugar

1 cup water or Milk

1 Egg, beaten

Mix together and add Yeast mixture.

Add 1 ½ cups Flour and beat hard

Add Flour (by the cup) to make a soft dough and mix well

Set in a warm place to rise. Make into rolls, allow to rise again, and bake at 350 degrees until golden brown.

Brandy Alexander

Dash of Grated Nutmeg

1 ounce Half and Half
Cubes

1 ½ ounces of Brandy

1 ounce of dark Crème de Cacao   Half glass of small Ice

Place ice in shaker, add Brandy, Crème de Cacao, Half and Half. Shake well. Strain mixture into glass and sprinkle with grated Nutmeg.

Bread Pudding with Whiskey Sauce

From my first taste of this incredible dessert to feeling completely blessed by actually eating the Brennans' "Bread Pudding Soufflé", absolutely nothing gets a higher grade for "incredibly good dessert" than Bread Pudding. I have collected a number of recipes for Bread Pudding; however, I can't get past this recipe to experiment with others. Any bread pudding recipe which does not start with raisins and include stale French bread and Whiskey could be risky to play around with.

PUDDING

½ cup Raisins	½ cup chopped Pecans
4 cups Milk	1 teaspoon Cinnamon
1 cup Heavy Cream	1 teaspoon Nutmeg
4 large Eggs	1 teaspoon Vanilla
1 ½ cups Sugar	1 stick Sweet Cream, Unsalted Butter
1 large stale loaf French Bread	6 Tablespoons for puding, 2 to Butter Baking Dish

Soak Raisins in small bowl of water for 2 – 3 hours, drain and discard water.

Combine Milk, Cream, Eggs, Sugar, Raisins and Pecans in a large bowl. Mix well. Add Cinnamon, Nutmeg and Vanilla.

Tear the French loaf into 2-4 inch pieces and add to the mixture.

Butter a 9 X 13 casserole or loaf pan and pour the bread mixture into the pan. Cut Butter in 6 equal pieces and press into the top of the loaf. Cook in a water bath in a 350 degree oven for an half hour, the transfer to oven rack and finish cooking another 30 – 45 minutes.

WHISKEY SAUCE

3 Eggs	½ cup Milk
1 cup Sugar	1 Tablespoon Cornstarch
1 teaspoon Vanilla	¼ cup cold Water
3 Tablespoons Canadian Whiskey	

Break Eggs in a large saucepan and whisk over medium heat until slightly thickened. Add Sugar, Vanilla and Milk and cook until hot. Do not boil. Mix Cornstarch in ¼ cup cold water.

Stir the cornstarch into the Egg mixture, stirring constantly. Add the Whiskey and cook the Sauce over medium heat until smooth and thick. About 15 minutes. Stir frequently. Serve the Whiskey Sauce chilled over slices of Bread Pudding.

CHRISTMAS EVE DINNER MENU #1

Appetizer

Oysters En Brochette
Chilled Champagne

Main Course

Fried turkey
Shrimp Gumbo
Crisp Roasted Garlic Bread Loaves

Dessert

Fresh Strawberries Dipped in Chocolate
Hot Coffee with Orange Liquor and Whipped Cream

Oysters en Brochette

16 strips of Bacon

2 cups Milk

Salt and White Pepper, to taste,
   Approximately 2 teaspoons each

1 dash Tabasco Sauce

36 large Oysters

1 Egg

2 cups Vegetable Oil

3 Lemon Wedges and 3 Lime Wedges seeded

2 cups Flour

Cut each strip of Bacon in half then panfry until cooked through but not crisp. Drain on paper towel. Arrange the Oysters and Bacon strips alternately on 6 skewers, placing half dozen Oysters and 6 pieces of Bacon on each.

Preheat the Oil in a pan large enough to lay each skewer flat.

In a medium mixing bowl, combine the Milk, Egg, Salt, Pepper and Tabasco to make a batter, whisking well. Then pour the batter into a glass dish with 2 inch sides. Pour the Flour onto a large sheet of aluminum foil. Dip the Brochettes into the batter to dredge. Then roll in Flour. Shake off excess Flour and set a few skewers at a time into the hot oil. Allow them to fry, turning frequently, until golden brown. Drain on brown paper, the transfer to a heated platter. Serve with Lemon and Lime wedges. Modify to accommodate number of guests.

MARKETLIST: Shrimp, Bacon, ten pound Turkey, Peanut Oil, Milk, Eggs, Tabasco, Oysters, Vegetable Oil, Lemons, Limes, Tabasco, Strawberries, Orange Liqueur, Whipping Cream, French Loaves, Garlic, Rosemary, Thyme, Oregano, Basil, Butter, Bay Leaves, Okra, Tomatoes, White and Green Onions, Celery, Strawberries, Chocolate Chips (melting), Flour, Cajun Injectors and Cajun Seasonings, Coffee, Champagne

Fried Turkey

To anyone unfortunate enough to never have tasted 'fried turkey', this recipe/procedure is printed especially for you. It is hoped that you will acquire the necessary equipment and supplies and proceed fearlessly to achieve preparation techniques of this very delicious and unique taste and have the skills to prepare Fried Turkey whenever you choose in the future.

The previous cooking methods required a propane tank to fuel a burner set in a steel framed rack and holding a pot large enough for the bird. The project had to be completed out of doors safely away from flammable materials and where possible oil spills would not cause injuries. A large 20 quart heavy pot can be used on an inside burner, however, extreme caution must be exercised to insure the correct amount and temperature of hot oil and lowering and removing the bird from the hot oil. The above methods and vessels could accommodate a 12 – 15 pound Turkey. There are electric "turkey fryers" available now which can accommodate a 10 pound bird and are safer to use in your kitchen.

1 Ten pound Turkey	Cajun Injectors – I like having several
Thawed, cleaned and neck and giblets	Liquid injectables (variety of seasonings)
Removed	You may wish to prepare your own
Peanut Oil , sufficient to cover the Turkey	injectable seasonings
during frying and according to fryer	Long metal hook to lower into pot, rotate
Instruction-1 and ½ - 2 Gallons	and remove Turkey

The day before frying the Turkey, clean, wash, remove giblets and place Turkey on large chopping block covered with heavy duty aluminum foil. Load the injectors with your choice of seasonings in Butter or oil and inject the needle into the bird at various locations including the thicker parts of the legs, thighs and Turkey breast. Rub a small amount of seasonings on the outside of the bird breast, thighs and back and wrap securely in the aluminum foil. Refrigerate overnight. Do not remove the metal brace at the large opening between turkey legs.

To fry, bring Peanut Oil to a 350 degree temperature. You will need a long needled thermometer to insure correct temperature is maintained. Remove aluminum foil, wipe the bird with damp paper towels to remove any residue, and gently lower into hot oil with the neck cavity entering the pot first. Fry for 40 – 50 minutes, rotating the turkey from time to time and monitoring the temperature to maintain 350 degrees.

Remove the bird from the oil by gently lifting the bird with the metal hook using the metal frame left inside the bird. Insure that additional support, i.e., long handled bar-b-cue fork, is used to assist in safely removing the bird from the hot oil. Place the bird on several layers of heavy duty aluminum foil, wrap securely to allow it to continue to cook for one hour before serving. Carve and serve the bird on a warm platter.

Allow the oil to cool before removing and cleaning pot.

Shrimp and Okra Gumbo

4-5 pounds medium Shrimp, peeled,
   Deveined, beheaded and rinsed
3 – 4 pounds fresh (small/tender) Okra
   Caps and tips removed and sliced thin
   (1/4 to ½)
4 cups fresh Tomatoes, (blanched,
   Peeled, seeded and chopped)
2 cups White Onion, chopped
1 bunch Celery, inside sticks, chopped
½ cup Vegetable Oil for frying (more if needed)

2 teaspoons Salt
1 teaspoon Thyme
1 teaspoon Cayenne
6-8 Bay Leaves
3-4 quarts Water

Heat oil in a large pot over medium-high heat. Fry the Okra, stirring constantly for 12-15 minutes until most of the slime disappears. Add Tomatoes, Onions and Celery. Cook until vegetables are soft and slime has completely disappeared, about 20 minutes. Add seasonings and water. Bring mixture a boil, then reduce heat to simmer for 20-30 minutes. Add the Shrimp, cook, stirring occasionally for 30 minutes. Remove Bay Leaves, serve with Crusty French Bread.

Crisp Roasted Garlic French Loaves

Purchase whole loaves of French Bread (fresh baked daily in many supermarket bakeries). With serrated knife, make diagonal cuts at 2 inch intervals for the length of the loaf. Insert chopped fresh garlic bits, sliced Butter pieces, sprinkles of Italian seasoning, or your mix of Thyme, Rosemary, Oregano, Basil into the cuts with the Garlic and Butter (do not use Margarine).   Wrap loaves in Aluminum Foil and bake for about 15 minutes. Open and remove foil, return loaves to oven, continue to bake and brown the loaves until crusty on top and sides. Serve with Shrimp Gumbo.

Fresh Strawberries Dipped in Chocolate

2 Large Boxes Fresh Strawberries
1 large bag Chocolate Chips (Nestles)
Rinse and drain on paper towels
(See directions for melting on package)
(do not remove leaves)

Melt chocolate and thoroughly dry berries. Cool Chocolate slightly and dip berries in Chocolate to coat. Place on waxed paper and place in refrigerator to cool and harden chocolate. When chilled, serve immediately. Other fruits including Apples, Pears and Oranges are excellent choices for dipping in Chocolate and serving as a light dessert.

CHRISTMAS EVE DINNER MENU #2

Appetizer

Platters of Crunchy Fried Vegetables
Red and Green Bell Peppers, Onion Rings, Mushrooms,
French Fries, Artichokes, Cauliflower
French Onion Dip
Spinach Dip
Avocado Dip

Main Course

Grilled Gourmet Pork and Cheese Stuffed Links
Seafood Quiche (Shrimp, Lobster)
Italian Sausage and Broccoli Quiche
Fruit Salad in Pineapple Halves
Drizzled with Poppy Seed Dressing
Chilled Sauvignon Blanc

Dessert

Santa's Chocolate Chunk Cookies with
Scoops of Vanilla Ice Cream and Chocolate Sauce

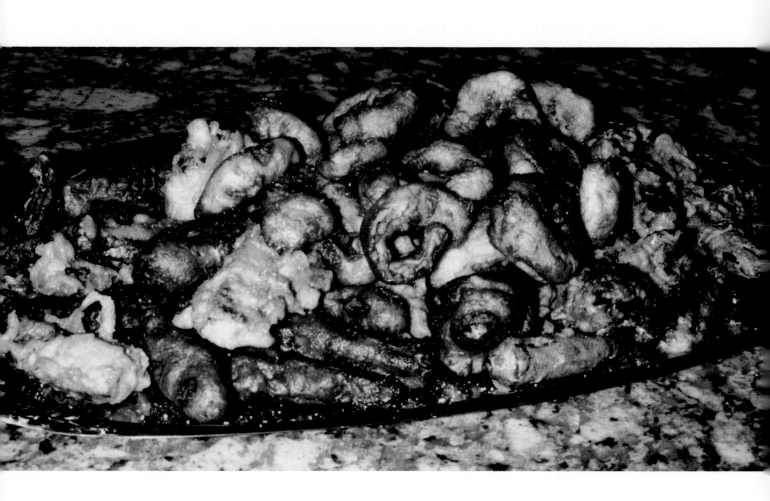

Platters of Crunchy Fried Vegetables

Two Red and two Green Bell Peppers
  Seeded, cleaned and sliced into 1" sliced
Two White Onions, peeled and sliced
  Into ½" slices
12 Mushrooms, Stems removed, cleaned
  And dried on paper towel
Sea Salt

4 Idaho Potatoes, peeled, cut into
  French Fry pieces
2 cans unseasoned Artichokes, drained
1 whole Cauliflower, clean and dry, cut
  into 2 – 3 inch flowers
Vegetable Oil for Frying

Vegetable Frying Batter

2 cups Flour
1 teaspoon Salt
1 1/3 cup water

¼ cup Oil
2 Egg Whites (beaten to stiff peaks)

In large mixing bowl, sift 2 cups Flour, add Salt, water and oil. With electric mixer, beat well until smooth. Add Egg Whites folding into flour mixture. Prepare deep fryer with Vegetable Oil for frying. Temperature should be 325 – 350 degrees. Dip vegetables into mixture and fry until crisp and golden brown. Do not dip Potatoes before deep frying. Remove vegetables with slotted spoon and drain on paper towels or brown paper. Sprinkle with salt, paprika, or other seasoning as desired. Serve immediately on large platters with variety dips.

French Onion Dip

1 16 oz container of Sour Cream

1 Package Lipton Onion Soup and Dry Mix

Mix dry mix into Sour Cream and chill until ready for use. Present in bowl set in large platter of crispy fried Vegetables and Potatoes. Note. This is a 'very simple' and delicious flavor to compliment your crispy vegetables. You may choose to serve it at room temperature.

Spinach Dip

1 package frozen chopped Spinach

   Thawed and placed in colander

    To remove all liquid

4 Green Onions, cleaned and shopped

¼ cup fresh chopped fresh Dill

1 Eight once container Sour Cream

2 Tablespoons Miracle Whip

½ cup chopped fresh Parsley

Sea Salt and fresh ground Black Pepper to taste

Mix Sour Cream and Miracle Whip until smooth. Add Spinach, Onions, Parsley, Dill and mix well. Add Salt and Pepper to taste. Chill and serve on large platter with crisp fried Vegetables, Potatoes and variety of dips.

Avocado Dip

2 large ripe Green or Black Avocados

   Peeled and mashed

1 Lime

½ pound thin sliced lean bacon

1 Sixteen ounce package Sour Cream

5 or 6 Green Onions, cleaned/chopped

½ cup Cilantro, chopped

Sea Salt to taste

Fry Bacon until crisp, crumble. Squeeze Lime Juice over peeled and mashed Avocados. Combine Avocados, Sour Cream, Green Onions, Cilantro and stir. Add crumbled crisp Bacon and Sea Salt to taste. Chill and serve in bowl on large platter of crisp fried Vegetables, Potatoes and various dips.

MARKET LIST: Gourmet Selection of Pork, Chicken and/or Cheese Links, White and Green Onions, Sour Cream, Cream Cheese, Cilantro, Bacon, Avocados, Limes, Shrimp, Lobster, Italian Sausage, Broccoli, Oranges, Bananas, Pineapple, Poppy Seed Dressing, Sauvignon Blanc, Mushrooms, Canned Artichokes, Red and Green Bell Peppers, Onion Soup Mix, Chocolate Bars, Vanilla Ice Cream, Chocolate Sauce, Frozen Broccoli, Frozen Spinach, Milk, Cream, Swiss Cheese, Cilantro, Fresh Dill, Fresh Parsley, Strawberries, Eggs, Vegetable Oil, Paprika

Grilled Gourmet Links (Various Fillings)

This Christmas Eve recommendation is included that you may enjoy a unique and flavor filled dining experience without the effort you will be expending in the kitchen for tomorrow's meal. There are a variety of unique Beef, Pork, Chicken, Cheese and Rice fillings available on today's market. For this Christmas Eve meal, grill your selections of "Links" and serve with the Seafood and Italian Sausage Quiche. The Quiche mix could be prepared earlier in the day and completed and baked just an hour before your Christmas Eve dining. The cookies are large cookies to be served as dessert with Ice Cream and Chocolate Sauce but can be left for Santa with a glass of cold Milk.

Pie Crusts for two 10 inch Quiche Bakers

3 Cups sifted Flour

1 ½ teaspoons Salt

1 cup plus 1 Tablespoon Solid Vegetable Shortening

6 Tablespoons Water

Mix Flour and Salt in large mixing bowl. Cut Shortening into Flour with pastry blender until mixture is very fine. Add half of water, stir, and add second half, blend well into mix. Divide and roll out on floured board or flat surface in circles large enough to accommodate a 10 inch Quiche Baker. Lightly flour bottom of Quiche pans and fold crusts into pans. Fold under any excess crust and crimp edges around outside of baker. Prick crust at various places with fork on sides and bottom of crust.

Seafood Quiche Filling

N O T E : Most recipes for Seafood Quiche recommend "Shrimp and Crabmeat". The use of Lobster meat, if available, in the filling is offered as a substitute or addition to Crabmeat as a result of the tendency of the Crabmeat to become less flavorful and shrink in the cooking process. There are a numerous recipes available for Seafood Quiche, however, this basic custard can be used to accommodate a variety of fillings. Experiment and enjoy.

1 cup Medium Shrimp, peeled, deveined and beheaded (cook about 3 minutes in boiling salted water and chop into 2" pieces

1 cup cooked Lobster, cut into 2 inch pieces

1 cup Crabmeat, drained

1 ½ teaspoons Flour

½ cup Chopped Green Bell Pepper

1 8 oz package Grated Cheddar Cheese

3 Eggs Beaten

2 ½ cups Light Cream

¼ teaspoon Cayenne Pepper

½ teaspoon Salt

½ cup Chopped Green Onion

Sprinkle of Paprika

Place Cheddar cheese, Bell Pepper, Green Onion, Shrimp, Lobster and Crabmeat (if used) in bottom of Quiche Dish. Mix Light Cream, Beaten Eggs, Flour, Cayenne Pepper and Salt and blend well. Pour over Cheese and Seafood and lightly sprinkle with Paprika. Bake on cookie sheet at 350 degrees until cooked through and is crust is brown and crisp. May be frozen and thawed and baked later.

Italian Sausage and Broccoli Quiche Filling

One 8 Oz box frozen Chopped Broccoli

1 6 oz package grated Swiss Cheese

1 6-8 oz package of Ground Italian Sausage

3 or 4 Green Onions, thinly sliced

¼ teaspoon Salt

¼ teaspoon Nutmeg

Dash Cayenne Pepper

1 ½ Tablespoons Flour

2 cups Light Cream

4 Eggs, lightly beaten

1 Unbaked Crust for 10 Inch
                    Quiche baking dish

Paprika

Brown Sausage in skillet, drain oil and set aside. Thaw Broccoli and press in colander to remove liquid.

In bottom of unbaked Quiche Crust, place Grated Swiss Cheese, Green Onions, Broccoli and Italian Sausage. Mix Cream, Eggs, Flour, Salt, Nutmeg and Pepper and pour over Sausage and Cheese. Lightly mix with Sausage and Cheese. Sprinkle with Paprika and bake in 350 degree oven for 35 - 45 minutes (or longer) until thoroughly cooked and crust is browned.

Fruit Salad in Pineapple

2 large fresh Pineapples

1 large box fresh Strawberries

3 Apples

4 Bananas

1 package miniature Marshmallows

1 cup flaked Cocoanut

2 cups heavy Whipping Cream

½ cup Sugar

1 teaspoon Vanilla

1 can Large Mixed Fruit

Poppy Seed Dressing

Cut Pineapples in half and remove centers, chop and put in large mixing bowl. Place the four pineapple halves in a circle, end to end, on large platter covered with lettuce leafs. Clean and remove leaves of Strawberries and cut in half, peel and core Apples, cut into 1 ½ inch chunks, peel and slice Bananas into 1 inch slices, and combine with Pineapple chunks. Mix fruit and add Cocoanut and Marshmallows. Drain canned Fruit and add to mixture.

Beat Whipping Cream and add Sugar and Vanilla. Mix Whipped Cream into Fruit mixture and spoon and mound into the Pineapple Halves. Drizzle with Poppy seed dressing if desired. Chill and serve.

Santa's Chocolate Chunk Cookies

2 ½ cups old fashioned Oats

2 cups all purpose Flour

1 teaspoon Baking Powder

1 teaspoon Baking Soda

½ teaspoon Salt

1 Cup (2 sticks) unsalted Butter
   Room temperature

4 ounces Milk Chocolate, grated

1 ½ cups Chopped Pecans

1 cup Sugar

1 cup firmly packed Golden Brown Sugar

2 Eggs

1 teaspoon vanilla Extract

12 ounces Semisweet Chocolate, cut
         into ½ inch chunks

Preheat oven to 350 degrees. Butter cookie sheets. In food processor, grind oats to fine texture. Transfer to a large mixing bowl. Add Flour, Baking Powder, Baking Soda and Salt to Oats and blend well. Using electric mixer, beat Butter and both Sugars in another large bowl until light and fluffy. Beat in Eggs and Vanilla. Mix in dry ingredients. Fold in Semisweet Chocolate, Pecans and Milk Chocolate.

Form cookie dough into 2 ½ inch balls. Place cookie dough on prepared cookie sheets and press lightly to spread dough, spacing dough about 3 inches apart. Bake cookies until golden and transfer to a rack to cool.

Serve cookies with scoops of Vanilla Ice Cream drizzled with Chocolate sauce.

A large cookie (or two) and glass of cold Milk can be left near the Christmas Tree for Santa.

CHRISTMAS EVE DINNER MENU #3

Appetizers

Cheese, Jalapeno and Beef Nachos
With Sour Cream and Pico De Gallo
Queso with Fried Corn Tortilla Chips
Deep Fried Battered Stuffed Jalapenos
Cold Mexican Beer

Main Course

Pork Tamales
Homemade Beef Chili with grated Four Mexican Cheese
And Chopped Green Onions and Sour Cream
Salsa Verde
Guacamole and Chips

Dessert

Pecan Pralines
Mexican Coffee

This very special menu for Christmas Eve is presented in my book to remember the hard working and caring Mexican workers and friends during those early years on the farm in South Texas. On Christmas Eve, packages of warm, freshly made Pork Tamales would be delivered in celebration of Christmas and family and they were always so incredibly delicious.

This Christmas Eve menu is included remembering you and all your kindnesses.

Nachos

1 pound package Ground Beef	Chopped Fresh Garlic
Black Pepper and Salt to taste	1 can Refried Beans
1 6 ounce package Sour Cream	Grated Mexican Four Cheese
1 Jar Nacho sliced Jalapeno Peppers	1 large bag Tortilla Chips

Fry Ground Beef, Garlic, Salt and Pepper until cooked through and browned. Open and heat refried beans in small sauce pan. Add Salt and Pepper and a few drops of water to thin.

Spread Tortilla Chips on a Cookie Sheet and cover evenly with Refried Beans, cooked Ground Beef, Mexican Four Cheese. Drain Nacho Sliced Jalapenos and spread over the Cheese. Preheat oven to 350 degrees and place Nachos in oven until cheese has melted and bubbly.

Transfer to warm serving dishes and serve with Pico de Gallo and dollops of Sour Cream.

Queso with Fried Corn Tortillas (Chips)

CHILI CON QUESO

1 cup Butter

½ cup finely chopped Onion

1 can (1 lb.) Tomatoes, undrained

1 ½ to 2 cans (4 ounce size) Green
    Chilies, drained and chopped

½ teaspoons Salt

1 pound Monterey Jack Cheese, cubed

½ cup Heavy Cream

Heat Butter in medium skillet. Sauté Onion until tender. Add Tomatoes, Chilies and Salt, mashing Tomatoes with fork. Simmer, stirring occasionally, for about 15 minutes. Add Cheese cubes and stir until Cheese is melted. Stir in Cream and cook, stirring constantly for 2 minutes. Remove from heat and let stand for 15 minutes. Serve in candle warmer casserole as dip for fried Corn Tortilla Chips.

Pork Tamales

Authentic Pork Tamales are currently available in all major supermarkets. A variety of other meat and seasonings are also available and offer selections for this delightful food encased in Corn Masa and Husks and steamed to heat and cook the fillings. They are best steamed on a rack over boiling, salted water and served with salsas, chilies, and Mexican Charro Beans.

Homemade Beef Chili with Grated Mexican Four Cheese

There have been some "ups and downs" but life has been so good that I have had a copy of Frank X. Tolbert's "A Bowl Of Red" to guide at least one element of life in Texas, trying to cook, enjoying eating, and acquiring at least some of the required ingredients for the making of a passable "Bowl of Red". It is expressly established that the book is Not a Cookbook, however, I fortunately have gleaned from the pages that "Texas Chili" is an edible version of "real Chili, the culinary salvation of Texicans. Here's a version sans questionable "innards, unacceptable and improperly prepared Chili Peppers, and an abbreviated cooking timetable (because sometimes we have to work too) for your preparation – (possible preparation).

2 ½ - 3 pounds of Beef cut into 1 - 1 ½ inch chunks - only Texas Black Angus range fed beef

1 large White Onion, chopped

1 stick Butter and ½ cup Vegetable Oil

4 cloves Garlic, chopped

1 roasted, peeled and chopped Ancho Chili

1 teaspoon ground Cumin

1 teaspoon Chili Powder

2 cans Tomato sauce with Tomato bits (canned Crushed Tomatoes can be used)

Brown Beef, Onion and Garlic in mixture of Butter and Vegetable Oil in a large (cast iron) skillet. Drain. Add Chili peppers, ground Cumin, Salt and Ground Pepper and Chili Powder. Cook on low heat to incorporate flavors. Stir in canned Tomato Bits, reduce heat simmer until thick. Top Chili with grated Mexican Four Cheese, Sour Cream and Chopped Green Onions.

SALSA VERDE (SEE PAGE 94)

GUACAMOLE AND CHIPS (SEE PAGE 94)

PICO DE GALLO (SEE PAGE 94)

Dessert

Pecan Pralines

6 cups Dark Brown Sugar

2 cups White Sugar

1 ½ cups Water

6 cups Pecans

Mix together Dark Brown Sugar, White Sugar and Water in large pot. With wooden spoon, cook and stir over Medium High heat until mixture reaches the soft ball stage. Remove from heat and add Pecans. Return pot to burner and cook and stir until mixture returns to a rolling boil. Remove from burner and beat with wooden spoon until candy becomes cloudy. Spread waxed paper on chop block and spoon candy onto waxed paper to cool working quickly to prevent candy from changing consistency. When all candy has been turned onto waxed paper, begin with the first candy Praline and move to a plate or platter to cool.

Serve this meal with a Coffee Liqueur of strong dark roasted Mexican Coffee served in ¾ filled cups and 2 o 3 Tablespoons of Capucino. Top with Whipped Cream.

MARKET LIST: Mexican Four Cheese, Corn tortillas, Sour Cream, Refried Beans, White and Green Onions, Pork Tamales, Ground Beef and Beef for Chili, Nacho Jalapeno Slices, Tomatoes with tomato Bits, Vegetable Oil, Butter, Fresh Garlic, Tortilla Chips, Capucino, Dark Brown Sugar, White Sugar, Pecans, Canned Green Chilis, Monterey Jack Cheese, Heavy Cream, ground Cumin, Fresh Garlic, Chili Powder, Ancho Chilies, Pinto Beans, Heavy Cream, Coffee

CHRISTMAS DAY MENU #1

Appetizer

Platter of Fried Seafood (Oysters, Shrimp and Scallops)
Served with Lemon and Lime Slices and Seafood Sauce
California Sparkling Wine

Main Course

Roast Goose with Northern Bread/Sage Dressing
Cream Gravy
Baked Mashed Potatoes with Grated Cheddar and Chives
Steamed Brussel Sprouts with Baby Carrots and Onions
Frozen Pineapple and Apricot Salad served on Leaf Lettuce
Australian Shiraz
Nesselrode Pie
Kahlua Coffee with Whipped Cream

Fried Seafood Platter

Batter Fried Shrimp and Oysters and Butter/Olive Oil Sauté of Sea Scallops

2 dozen fresh gulf jumbo Shrimp

    Heads removed, peeled and deveined

2 dozen fresh Oysters, shucked

1 dozen medium Sea Scallops

Vegetable Oil for Frying

8 ounces (2 sticks sweet cream Butter

        and 4-6 Tablespoons Olive Oil

1 teaspoon Paprika

BATTER FOR FRYING SHRIMP AND OYSTERS

3 cups Flour

2 Twelve ounce cans Beer

2 cups Flour (spread on aluminum foil)

This simple batter is excellent for deep frying seafood. Mix the batter and set aside for 2-3 hours. Clean and prepare Shrimp and Oysters. Spread 2 cups flour on aluminum foil. Heat Oil to 350 degrees in deep pot. Roll Shrimp in flour, then dip in batter mix, then roll again in flour. Fry until brown and crisp. Lift from oil with slotted spoon. Drain on Paper towels, serve immediately.

VEGETABLE OIL SAUTE FOR SEA SCALLOPS

In a non-stick skillet, heat one stick of Butter and 4 Tablespoons of Olive Oil.

Sprinkle Paprika over Scallops and sauté in medium hot oil. Do not batter Scallops. Turn only once with a metal spatula and cook until done through. Add Butter and oil as needed. Sprinkle with Paprika and serve immediately. Serve Shrimp, Oysters and Scallops on heated platter with slices of Lemons and Limes and varieties of Seafood Sauces.

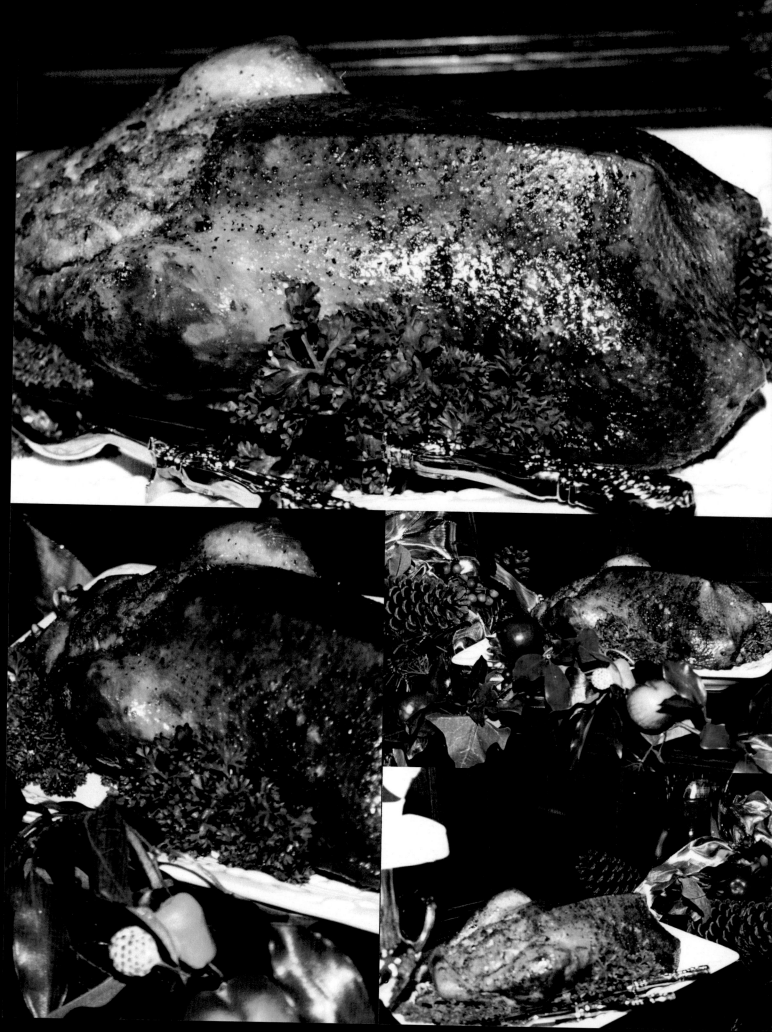

Roast Goose with Northern Bread/Sage Dressing

Roast Goose – Select a large 10-12 pound Goose (you will only be able to find them frozen and ordinarily in specialty food markets. Thaw and pre-cook the Goose for about 2 hours in a moderate oven under a foil cover. Remove from heat and drain off fat.

Northern Bread/Sage Stuffing

2 loaves of sliced white bread, toasted and torn or cut into 1-2 inch pieces

2 cloves of Garlic, chopped

3-4 Tablespoons Rubbed Sage

1 white Onion, chopped

2 baking Apples, peeled, cored, chopped

1 cup Chicken Stock (use only enough liquid to lightly moisten)

NOTE: May add sausage to the stuffing. Sauté Sausage, drain and add to stuffing mixture.

Mix all ingredients, do not add Butter or oils and stuff the partially cooked bird. Generously rub fresh groun black pepper into the bird and pierce the skin in several places to release oil during baking. Bake Goose approximately 2 additional hours and baste with pan drippings.

Cream Gravy

½ cup Flour

Pan drippings from roasting Goose

1 cup of whole Milk

1 cup Water

Salt and Pepper

Brown Flour in pan drippings (add flour as needed) to a light tan color. Add mixture of Milk and Water gradually, continue cooking until desired consistency for Gravy, season with Salt and Pepper and serve in heated/warm gravy boat.

Baked Mashed Potatoes

6 – 8 Idaho Potatoes	3 cups Water
½ cup Milk	1 4 ounce stick Sweet Cream Butter
4-6 Chopped Green Onions	Salt and fresh ground Black Pepper
1 4 ounce stick Sweet Cream Butter	1 8 ounce Package Grated Cheddar

Peel Potatoes, chop into 2 – 3 inch squares and cook in boiling, salted water until soft. Mash Potatoes, add Milk, Butter, Salt and Pepper and half the chopped green onions. Place half of Potatoes in a shallow Buttered casserole, stir in half the Grated Cheddar and remaining Chives. Top with remaining Potatoes and Cheddar. Gently mix, bake until Golden Brown.

Tiny Steamed Vegetables with Brown Sugar Glaze

2 packages (about 10 – 15 Shallots)

1 bag gourmet fingerling Potatoes (Red and White)

12 Boiler Onions

1 small bag Baby Carrots

½ pound Green Beans (2" long)

3-4 Tablespoons Brown Sugar

1 Tablespoon Sugar

1 4 oz stick sweet cream Butter

1 box Brusssel Sprouts

Clean and peel (as needed) all vegetables. Prepare large pot with Steamer rack. Cook Potatoes and Shallots until just tender. Add Green Beans and Baby Carrots and Boiler Onions. Steam for another 10 – 15 minutes or until tender and add Brussel Sprouts and Green Beans. Steam all vegetables until just tender. Remove from Steamer basket and put in large bowl with lid or cover with aluminum foil. In small sauce pan, mix together Butter, Sugar and Brown Sugar. Heat and stir until liquid. Pour over vegetables and toss lightly. Sprinkle with Sea Salt and surround Roast goose on large serving platter.

Frozen Pineapple And Apricot Salad

1 cup Miracle Whip Salad Dressing

8 oz. can Pineapple Chunks, drained

½ cup Maraschino Cherries

Red food coloring

1 cup Heavy Cream, Whipped

1 8 Oz package Cream Cheese

8 ¾ oz can Apricot Halves, drained, chopped

2 Tablespoons Confectioner's Sugar

2 cups Kraft Miniature Marshmallows

Mix together Salad Dressing and Cream Cheese (softened) until blended. Stir in Fruit, Sugar and a few drops of Red Food Coloring. Fold in Marshmallows and Whipped Cream. Pour mixture into a 9 x 5 inch loaf pan and freeze. Unmold 30 minutes before serving, place on cake serving dish over a bed of leaf lettuce.

MARKET LIST: Shrimp, Oysters, Scallops, Lemons, Limes, Seafood Sauces, Sparkling Wine, Goose, 10-12 pounds, Loaf Bread, Sausage (if desired), White and Green Onions, Olive Oil, Vegetable Oil, Butter, Paprika, Beer, Flour, Milk, Potatoes, Grated cheddar Cheese, Sage, Apples, Chicken Stock, Garlic, Candied Fruit, Sugar, Unflavored Gelatin, Whipping Cream, canned Pineapple Chunks, canned Apricot Halves, Confectioner's Sugar, Miracle Whip Salad Dressing, Maraschino Cherries, Red Food Coloring, Miniature Vegetables, Carrots, Green Beans, Shallots, Gourmet Fingerlings, Brussel Sprouts, Boiler Onions, Brown Sugar, Cream Cheese, Candied Fruit, Unflavored Gelatin, Rum, Shiraz, Kahlua and Coffee

Nesselrode Pie

9 inch Baked Pie Shell – see Pie shell recipe- page_____

1 8ounce container diced mixed Candied Fruit

5 Tablespoons Rum

4 Eggs Separated

1 ¼ cups Milk

¾ cups Sugar

1 envelope unflavored Gelatin

¼ teaspoon Salt

1 cup heavy or Whipping Cream

Prepare early in day or a day ahead. In a small bowl, mix ½ cup Candied Fruit with 2 Tablespoons Rum, cover and reserve for garnish later

In heavy 2 quart saucepan with wire whisk, beat Egg Yolks, Milk and Sugar until well mixed. Sprinkle Gelatin evenly over Egg mixture. Over medium-low heat, cook until Gelatin is completely dissolved and mixture is thickened and coats spoon, about 20 minutes.

In a large bowl with mixer at high speed, beat Egg Whites and Salt until stiff peaks form, set aside. In small bowl, using same beaters, with mixer at medium speed, beat Heavy Cream until stiff peaks form.

With wire whisk, gently fold Egg Yolk mixture, whipped cream and remaining Candied Fruit into Egg-white mixture. Spoon into Pie Crust, refrigerate until set, about 2 hours.

Garnish with reserved Candied Fruit mixture.

CHRISTMAS DAY DINNER MENU #2

Appetizer

Stuffed Oysters
Blender Frozen Mimosas
Salad
Winter Salad Greens with Vinaigrette

Main Course

Crown Roast of Pork with Apricot and Prune Stuffing
Baked White Onions with Crisp Bacon and Pimento
Roast Sweet Potatoes with Pecan Caramel Sauce
Burgundy Wine
Apricot Tea
High Rise Dinner Rolls
Maitre d Butter

Dessert

Bananas Foster
Kahlua Coffee

Stuffed Oysters

2 Dozen Fresh Oysters on the half shell

¼ cup chopped Green Onion

½ cup hot water (if needed)

½ teaspoon Rubbed Sage

½ cup Oyster Water

2 cups Corn Bread (made ahead)

¼ cup chopped White Onion

¼ cup chopped Celery

½ teaspoon Black Pepper

This delicious Oyster dish was served as an appetizer in a famous Houston seafood restaurant. The waitress was kind enough to explain what she knew as to the preparation method. I use the Louisiana Oyster, however, depending upon your part of the country, the Goose Point or other thick and salty Oyster should be delicious with this dressing.

Chop Onions and Celery very fine. Break up the Corn Bread and add all ingredients. Add only enough water to moisten the Corn Bread. Place the Oysters in the shell on a large cookie sheet and top each with a rounded Tablespoon of Corn Bread Dressing. Bake at 350 degrees until the dressing is brown and juice of the Oyster is bubbling. Do not overcook Oysters.

Serve with Lemon and Lime Wedges and Tabasco Sauce.

NOTE: See Blender Mimosa Recipe - Page 58

Winter Salad Greens with Vinaigrette

DRESSING

½ cup Extra Virgin Olive Oil

¼ cup White Wine Vinegar

¼ cup fresh squeezed Grapefruit Juice

GREENS

4 cups broken Green Winter Lettuce

2 cups broken Arugula

2 cups baby Spinach Leaves

Salt and Pepper

Place all greens in a large salad bowl. Whisk the Oil, Vinegar and Grapefruit Juice until slightly thickened. Sprinkle Sea Salt and freshly ground Black Pepper over leaves and drizzle oil and vinegar mixture and toss to cover all greens.

Crown Roast of Pork with Apricot and Prune Stuffing

Select an 8 – 10 pound Pork Crown Roast. Stand roast in baking dish with bone ends up and wrap bones in aluminum foil to prevent overbrowning during the cooking process. Insure center area allows

1 cup chopped Prunes

½ cup chopped White Onion

½ teaspoon Rubbed Sage

1 4 oz bar Sweet Cream Butter

1 cup chopped dried Apricots

1 teaspoon Rosemary leaves

4-6 leaves fresh Rosemary

1 cup Madeira

Soak Prunes and Apricots in Madeira for 30 minutes. Combine with Onion, Rosemary, Sage and 2 oz of Melted Butter. Set aside. Prepare roasting pan with double layer of aluminum foil and set Roast on rack in shallow roasting pan and roast for approximately 2 and ½ hours to 3 hours. When temperature reaches 125 degrees on a meat thermometer, remove from oven and fill with Apricot and Prune mixture. Drizzle with remaining Butter. Cover filled roast with aluminum foil and return to oven. Cook until stuffing is hot and cooked through and roast has reached a temperature of 155 to 160 degrees. Serve on a round heated platter surrounded by green Parsley, baked filled Onions, fresh Rosemary Leaves and Apricots. Remove aluminum foil on bone ends and replace with white frills. Remove stuffing to a bowl and slice each rib to serve.

Baked White Onions with Crisp Bacon and Pimento

12 small White Onions

1 large jar chopped Pimento

1 pound lean Bacon (cut into 1 to 2" pieces

Salt and Pepper

Select medium to small white onions. Remove outer skins, cut ¼ inch off top of each onion, remove approximately ½ of onion center and set aside. Chop the removed centers and place in skillet with Bacon. Sauté Bacon and Onion until Bacon is crisp. Remove and drain on paper towels. Combine chopped Pimento with Bacon and Onion and season with Sea Salt and freshly ground Black Pepper. Fill each Onion with mixture and bake at 350 degrees until onions are fork tender. Circle Crown Pork Roast with fresh Rosemary, Onions, Parsley and Apricots.

Roasted Sweet Potatoes with Pecan Caramel Sauce

Select Medium Size and well-rounded Sweet Potatoes. Scrub and bake Potatoes until crisp outside and soft to the squeeze.

Prepare Dressing in advance.

1 cup Brown Sugar

½ cup Sugar

½ cup White Corn Syrup

1 cup chopped Pecans or Walnuts

½ stick Butter

½ bag white Miniature Marshmallows (2-3 cups)

1 Tablespoon Vanilla

Melt Marshmallows in a medium sauce pan over low heat, stirring constantly. Add Sugar, Brown Sugar, Butter and Corn Syrup. Stir and cook until all ingredients are melted and mixture is thick and clear. Bring to a boil, reduce heat. Add Vanilla and Pecans or Walnuts. Cook for another 5 minutes until Pecans are heated through. Serve in a candle heated or canned heat small server as dressing for roasted Sweet Potatoes. Slice Potatoes down center and fill with spoons of Marshmallow dressing.

Maitre d Butter

2 4 oz sticks Sweet Cream Butter, softened

½ cup chopped fresh Parsley

1 cup crushed ice with ½ cup bowl water

Mix Butter and Parsley and place in ice water. Spoon by rounded Tablespoons and form into round balls. Place on lettuce leaves on Serving Platter and refrigerate until ready to serve.

Bananas Foster (Brennan's New Orleans)

This is a very special way to please your guests at Christmastime. The recipe is a close second to the beautiful presentation at Brennan's, performed here by novices and with best of intentions for guest enjoyment.

¼ cup Butter

½ cup Brown Sugar, firmly packed

4 – 5 ripe Bananas, peeled, cut in halves lengthwise

¼ teaspoon Cinnamon

½ cup Sugar

1/2 cup White Rum

Vanilla Ice Cream

Combine Sugar and Cinnamon. In a chafing dish, melt Butter and add Brown Sugar. Lay Bananas in dish and sauté in Sugar mixture. Turn to cover both sides of Bananas. Sprinkle Bananas with Sugar/Cinnamon mix. Gently pour Rum into chafing dish and tilt slightly to include all Bananas. Carefully light Rum with long handled match or butane fuel igniter. Baste Bananas until flame burns out and serve with scoops of Vanilla Ice Cream.

High Rise Yeast Rolls

Note: See Recipe for High Rise Yeast rolls, Page 46

Kahlua Coffee

1 cup Fresh Hot Coffee

1 Tablespoon Cocoa (spread on saucer)

2 ounces Kahlua

1 ounce Amaretta (spread on saucer)

1 cup Whipped Cream

Dip the rim of a thick heat proof Glass in about 1 ounce of Kahlua, then press it into the Tablespoon of Cocoa. Put 1 ounce of Amaretta and remaining Kahlua in Glass. Fill with hot coffee, top with whipped cream.

MARKET LIST: Crown Pork Roast, White Wine Vinegar, Olive Oil, Grapefruit Juice, Winter Lettuce Arugula, Baby Spinach Leaves, Cocoa, Kahlua, Amaretta, Whipping Cream, Prunes, Apricots, Small White Onions, Bacon, Rosemary, Sage, Butter, Bacon, Sweet Potatoes, Pecans, Brown Sugar, Pimento, Corn Syrup, Vanilla, White Rum, Bananas, Cinnamon, Burgandy, Flour, Celery, Oysters, Corn Bread, Pie Shell, Unflavored Gelatin, Milk, Candied Fruit, Eggs

CHRISTMAS DAY DINNER MENU #3

Appetizer

Stuffed Baby Brie En Croute with Fruit
Brandy

Main Course

Herb Crusted Prime Rib with Port Wine Sauce
Potatoes Anna
Green Bean Casserole (traditional recipe)
Corn and Winter Squash with Bacon
Cabernet Sauvignon

Dessert

Ice Cream Pie
Hot Tea with Lemons

Stuffed Baby Brie en Croute

1 wheel (1 pound, 1 ounce) Baby Brie, Chilled

4 thin slices Capicolla or Baked Ham

8 thin slices Pastrami

1 Egg beaten with 1 Tablespoon Water

¼ pound Prosciutto, thinly sliced

1 sheet frozen Puff Pastry (commercially available)

Using a large sharp knife, cut chilled Brie horizontally into three layers. Arrange Capicolla on the bottom piece. Place middle layer of Brie on top and layer with Pastrami. Top with last piece of Brie; wrap in sliced Prosciutto. Cover and chill. Thaw puff pastry 20 minutes; unfold and roll on a lightly floured surface to a 14 inch square. Trim to a 14 inch circle and reserve the pastry trimmings. Place unwrapped Brie in center of pastry, brush pastry edges with Egg mixture. Fold pastry over the Brie. Trim edges as needed to enclose the Cheese. Place on a baking sheet, seam side down and brush with more egg mixture. Garnish with pastry trimmings and brush trimmings with egg and bake at 375 degrees for 25 minutes or until pastry is puffed and golden brown. Remove from oven and transfer to a wire rack and cool for at least 30 minutes before serving in order to assure Brie is firm. Serve with Sliced Pears, Apples and Spiced Peaches.

MARKET LIST: Wheel of Baby Brie, Prosciutto, Puff Pastry, Pastrami, Baked Ham, Butternut Squash, Baby Spinach, Frozen Corn, White and Green Onions, Bacon, Fresh Basil, Ice Cream, Cream of Tartar, Sugar, Vanilla, Prime Rib Roast, Irish Potatoes, Lemons, Port Wine, Apples, Peaches, Pears, Fresh Parsley, Rosemary, Thyme, Cornstarch, Garlic, Green Beans, Cream of Mushroom Soup, French Fried Onions, Milk, Eggs

Herb Crusted Prime Rib with Port Wine Sauce

1 Tablespoon Coarsely Ground Black Pepper

1 Tablespoon chopped Fresh Parsley

2 teaspoons chopped Fresh Rosemary

4 cups broth reduced to 1 cup

1 teaspoon chopped fresh Thyme

1 teaspoon minced Garlic

1 teaspoon Salt

7-8 pound oven-ready Prime Rib Roast

2 cups Ruby Port

2 teaspoons Cornstarch

2 teaspoons Water

Preheat oven to 350 degrees. In a bowl, combine Pepper, Parsley, rosemary, thyme, Garlic and Salt and mix well. Set Roast on a cutting board and rub mixture evenly over entire surface of meat. Place meat on a rack in a roasting pan and cook until an instant read thermometer inserted into the meat registers 120-125 degrees for very rare to medium rare about 2-2 ¼ hours, 130-135 degrees for medium to medium well, about 2 ¼ - 2 ¾ hours. Let meat rest 15-20 minutes before carving.

In a saucepan over medium-low heat, combine Port and broth, cook, stirring until liquid is reduced to 1 cup (10-12 minutes). Skim fat from roasting pan, set pan over medium-low heat, add Port mixture. In a bowl, whisk together Corn Starch and water and add to pan. Bring to a simmer, whisking constantly, until thickened, 4 – 6 minutes. Serve with Prime Rib.

Potatoes Anna

I am not sure what the origin of this preparation technique for Irish Potatoes is, but it has been a favorite of mine for as long as I can remember cooking. Peel and slice Potatoes, Butter a baking dish (I prefer a well seasoned cast iron skillet), layer the potatoes topped with Butter slices and sprinkling Salt and Pepper on each layer. Continue for three or four layers, cover and put in a hot (400 degree) oven for 45 minutes. Remove the cover, invert the skillet onto a warm serving platter. The Potatoes should be crisp and brown on top and creamy and soft toward the center.

Green Bean Casserole (Traditional)

7-8 cups cooked Green Beans

2 cans Cream of Mushroom Soup

3 cups French Fried Onions

1 cup Milk

Stir Beans, Soup, Milk, and 1 and ½ cups Onions together and place in a Buttered 9 X 12 Casserole which can be brought to the table. Bake for 25-30 minutes at 350 degrees. Stir and add remaining French Fried Onions. Bake until onions are golden brown. Serve from the Casserole.

Corn and Winter Squash with Bacon

2 – 3 pounds Butternut Squash, peeled,
    Seeded and cut into 1/3 inch pieces
1 ½ 6 ounce packages Baby Spinach Leaves
1 16 ounce package Frozen Corn Kernals, thawed
2 cups chopped Onions
1 pound package lean Bacon
¼ cup chopped fresh Basil

Sauté Bacon in large pot until crisp, about ten minutes. Add Onions and Squash. Sauté until Squash is almost tender, about 12 minutes. Add Spinach and Corn. Heat and toss until Spinach wilts and corn is heated through, about another 5 minutes. Stir in Basil, season with Salt and Pepper. Serve hot.

Ice Cream Pie

Topping off the list of the very easiest of Christmas recipes, hopefully you will enjoy the holiday as much as your guests. This is the easiest of easy and is absolutely cherished by the children in the family.

1 baked pie shell
1 ½ gallon the family favorite ice cream flavor
6 Egg Whites (at room temperature)
½ - 1 teaspoon Cream of Tartar
½ - ¾ cup Sugar
1 teaspoon Vanilla

Separate Eggs and place Egg Whites in medium mixing bowl.

Beat Egg Whites with electric mixer and add Cream of Tartar and Sugar gradually, beating

until stiff peaks form. Add Vanilla and continue beating to incorporate Vanilla.

Soften Ice Cream slightly and dip by large spoon placing gently in baked pie shell. Spread until all of shell has been covered and press gently – do not break baked shell.

Spread Meringue over Ice Cream immediately and place in a hot 375 degree oven on the middle rack. Monitor browning of meringue and remove from oven to freezer when brown.

Soften for 5 – 10 minutes (if hard frozen) before serving. Slice and serve in pie sliced shapes with hot tea or coffee.

HANUKKAH CELEBRATION

Appetizer
Mini Polenta Cakes with Smoked Salmon

Main Course
Large Roasting Hen
Oven Roasted Beef Brisket
Rice Pilaf with Raisins
Steamed, Buttered Baby Carrots
Potatoes latkes
Challah

Hanukkah Sufganiyot (Doughnuts)

Mini Polenta Cakes with Smoked Salmon

1 cup Yellow Cornmeal

2 teaspoons Butter

1 clove Garlic, minced

2 1/3 cups low salt Chicken Broth

½ cup low-fat Buttermilk

¼ cup grated Parmesan Cheese

1 cup frozen Whole Kernel Corn, thawed

1/3 cup chopped Onion

3 Egg Whites

1 Egg

Fresh Dill Sprigs (optional)

¼ teaspoon Salt

¼ teaspoon White Pepper

¼ teaspoon Ground Red Pepper

Vegetable Cooking Spray

l/1 cup Nonfat Cream Cheese, softened

2 Tablespoons plain Nonfat Yogurt

1 teaspoon grated Lemon Rind

dash of Salt

3 ounces Cold Smoked Salmon cut into 20 two and ½ inch strips

Combine Cornmeal, Margarine and Garlic in large saucepan. Gradually add broth, stirring constantly with a wire whisk. Bring to a boil and reduce heat to medium. Cook 3 minutes or until thickened, stirring constantly. Remove from heat, stir in Buttermilk and Parmesan Cheese, and set aside.

Place the Corn and Onion in a food processor and process until Corn is coarsely chopped. Combine corn mixture, Egg Whites and Egg in a large bowl; stir well. Stir in Cornmeal mixture, ¼ teaspoon Salt and Pepper. Pour Polenta mixture into an 11 X 7 inch baking dish coated with cooking spray, spreading evenly. Bake at 400 degrees for 50 minutes or until browned. Let mixture cool. Cut corn mixture into 20 decorative shapes with a 1 ½ inch cutter. Remove shapes from baking dish and arrange on a baking sheet coated with cooking spray. Discard remaining Polenta mixture. Bake at 400 degrees for 20 minutes.

Combine non-fat Ceram Cheese, Yogurt, Grated Lemon Rind and Dash of Salt in a small bowl, stir well and set aside. Spoon about ¼ teaspoon Cream Cheese mixture onto each Polenta cake and top each cake with a Salmon Strip. Garnish with fresh Dill, if desired.

Grilled Salmon Steaks with Tarragon Sauce

STEAKS

4 (Eight Ounce) Salmon Steaks

2 Tablespoons Reduced fat Mayonnaise

2 Tablespoons dried Tarragon

1 Tablespoon Fresh Lemon Juice

Lemon Slices

TARRAGON SAUCE

2 Tablespoons plain low fat Yogurt

2 Tablespoons reduced fat Mayonnaise

1 ½ teaspoon Dried Tarragon

½ teaspoon Dijon Mustard

Combine all sauce ingredients and chill.

Spread Steaks with Mayonnaise and sprinkle with Tarragon. Grill, with grill lid closed, over medium-high heat (350 – 400 degrees) for ten minutes or until Salmon flakes easily with a fork. Sprinkle with Lemon Juice; serve with Tarragon Sauce and Lemon Slices.

Potato Latkes

4 medium sized Potatoes (Shredded)

6 Green Onions, cleaned, end tips
   removed and Chopped

2 Eggs, lightly beaten

Vegetable Oil for Frying

Sea Salt and Fresh Ground Black Pepper

2 Tablespoons Butter, melted

2/3 cups Flour

6 Ounces Sour Cream

Applesauce

Combine all ingredients except Vegetable Oil. Heat 1 (scant) Tablespoon of Vegetable Oil in a heavy non-stick skillet. Place a large spoonful of Potato mixture into heated skillet, press to form a circle and repeat with sufficient potatoes to fill the skillet. Cook until browned, turn once. When both sides are browned and potatoes are cooked through, move to a heated platter, drain on brown paper and continue until all pancakes are cooked. Serve with Applesauce, Sour Cream and Chopped Green Onions.

Roast Chicken

Large Roasting Hen, thawed, rinsed and
   Giblets removed

Sea Salt and Fresh Coarse Ground Black Pepper

2 Tablespoons Ground Sage

1 Medium White Onion, chopped

2 Tablespoons Chopped fresh Tarragon

Rub large cavity with Salt, Pepper, Tarragon and Sage. Place half the chopped Onion in the cavity with seasonings. Place Hen in large roasting pan and rub remaining seasonings on bird. Sprinkle chopped Onions in pan . Roast bird in 350 degree oven for 2 hours, basting frequently with cooking juices. Cover with an aluminum foil tent if needed to prevent over browning and cook until bird is cooked through.

Oven Roasted Brisket

Five to Six pound Beef Brisket

2 Cloves chopped Garlic

½ teaspoon Thyme

½ cup Olive Oil

Salt and Pepper

½ teaspoon Oregano

2 large Onions, sliced

1 large can crushed tomatoes

Wash, pat dry and place Brisket in roasting pan. Mix Seasonings and Olive Oil and rub over Brisket. Allow seasonings to remain on meat surface for an hour or two before cooking. Before cooking, cover top of Brisket with Onion slices and top with Tomatoes. Bake for 3 – 4 hours at 300 – 325 degrees in an aluminum foil covered baker. Remove cover and baste with drippings frequently during baking.

Glazed Baby Carrots

Purchase whole ready to eat baby Carrots, large package

Approximately 4 cups

2-3 cups water in Steamer, fitted with rack

1 small Jar Orange Marmalade

1 teaspoon Sea Salt

2 Tablespoons Brown Sugar

1 Tablespoon Sugar

½ teaspoon Ginger

Heat water over hot fire to a boil, reduce heat, place steamer rack on pan and fill with Baby Carrots. Cook/steam until carrots are just tender. Turn into an oven proof bowl. Mix Marmalade, Brown Sugar, Sugar, Ginger and Salt and spread over Carrots. Toss until thoroughly covered and Bake/keep warm in oven proof dish until ready to serve.

Rice Pilaf with Light and Dark Raisins

1 ½ cups Raw Rice

1 ½ cup water

½ stick Butter

½ teaspoon Oregano

½ cup each Light Raisins and Dark Raisins

1 large onion, chopped fine

1 teaspoon Salt

½ teaspoon Thyme

Mix all ingredients. Pour into Buttered 2 quart casserole. Bake at 350 degrees tightly covered for 1 hour and 30 minutes. Uncover and stir once lightly. Cover, bake 30 more minutes.

Challah Bread

5 ½ cups Flour

1 packages Active Dry Yeast

2 Tablespoons Sugar

1 cup warm water

1 teaspoon Salt

5 Eggs

1/3 cup Butter

1 Egg White

1 Tablespoon Water

Poppy Seeds

Flour Mixture. Combine 2 cups of Flour, Sugar, Salt and Yeast, mix well. Combine 1 cup Water and 1/3 cup Butter and heat over medium heat until Butter is melted – 130 degrees.

Combine warm liquid and 5 whole Eggs with the Flour mixture. Beat with an electric mixer until blended. Increase mixer speed and beat at medium until thoroughly blended. Add remaining flour and mix to make a bread dough.

Turn dough out onto a floured chop board and knead in an additional cup of Flour until dough is smooth and elastic. Place dough in a greased bowl, turn to grease all sides, cover with plastic wrap and let rise in a warm place until dough has doubled in size.

Punch down the dough two or three times to remove all air bubbles. Divide in half and roll into two 6 by 14 inch triangles. Cut each triangle lengthwise into three 14 X 2 inch strips. Grease cookie sheet and braid the three dough strips together producing two woven loaves. Let rise again until dough is doubled in size. Bake in a 400 degree oven. At about 10 minutes, remove from heat, baste the surface with a mix of the Egg White and 1 Tablespoon of water. Sprinkle Poppy Seeds on the loaf and bake another 10 – 15 minutes until loaf sounds hollow when tapped.

Hanukkah Sufganiyot

2 Tablespoons Active Dry Yeast

2 ½ cups all purpose Flour

2 large Eggs

½ teaspoon fresh grated Nutmeg

2 teaspoons Salt

1 cup Seedless Raspberry Jam

¼ cup plus 1 Tablespoon Sugar

(add more for rolling)

2 Tablespoons Unsalted Butter

@ room temperature

3 cups Vegetable Oil, plus more for bowl

Combine Yeast, ½ cup warm water, 1 teaspoon Sugar. Set aside until foamy, about 1 minutes.

Place Flour in large bowl. Make a well, add Eggs, Yeast mixture, ¼ cup Sugar, Butter, Nutmeg and Salt. With a wooden spoon stir until sticky dough forms. Turn dough out onto floured surface and knead until smooth, about 8 - 0 minutes. Place in Buttered bowl, cover with plastic wrap and let rise until doubled in bulk — 1 - ½ hours.

Roll dough out on a lightly floured surface to ¼ inch thick. Using a ½ inch round cutter, cut 20 rounds. Cover with plastic wrap, let rise 15 minutes.

Heat Vegetable Oil in a deep fryer to 370 degrees registers on a candy thermometer. Using a slotted spoon, drop dough rounds into hot oil and fry each side until brown. Drain on paper towel . Roll in Sugar while warm. Fit a pastry bag with plain tip and fill with Jam. Fill doughnuts with about 2 teaspoons of Jam.

MARKET LIST: Large Roasting Hen, Uncooked Salmon, Smoked Salmon, Beef Brisket, Cornmeal, Butter, Garlic, Frozen Corn, Eggs, Fresh Dill, White and Green Onions, White Pepper, Cream Cheese, Yogurt, Lemons, Oranges, White long grain Rice, White and Dark Raisins, Baby Carrots, Irish Potatoes, Flour, Vegetable Oil, Sour Cream, Fresh Tarragon, Thyme, Oregano, Olive Oil, Ground Sage, Baby Carrots, Canned Tomatoes, Yeast, Nutmeg, Buttermilk, Parmesan Cheese, Chicken Broth, Whole Kernel Corn, Applesauce, Low fat Yogurt, Ground Red Pepper

KWANZA CELEBRATION MENU

Appetizer

Coconut Chicken Fingers

Main Course

Smothered Pork Chops & Gravy
Brown Rice
Fried Okra Salad
Coconut Sweet Potato Casserole
Skillet Corn Bread
Cinnamon Tea

Baked Bananas
Caribbean Fudge Pie

Chocolate Drink with Whipped Cream
Hot Cocoa

I began the research for this section of the book several years ago and my appreciation for the foods included, as I've prepared and enjoyed them, has become immense. If you have not tasted Coconut Chicken Fingers dipped in Apricot Sauce, Skillet Corn Bread (warm with Butter) or Fudge Pie, it will be worth every minute of your preparation time to experience these very special flavors. Some of the more popular and frequently prepared Kwanza celebration dishes are included in this book, however, there is a wealth of information on line to expand your Kwanza culinary experiences. Enjoy!

Coconut Chicken Fingers with Apricot Dipping Sauce

1 ½ - 2 Pounds Boneless Chicken Breasts

2 Large Eggs - Beaten

1/3 Cup Butter, melted

½ teaspoon Garlic Powder

1 cup flaked Coconut

1 cup Flour

1 teaspoon Salt

½ teaspoon fresh ground Black Pepper

Rinse Chicken Breasts and cut into 1- ½ inch strips, set aside. Heat oven to 400 degrees.

Mix seasonings with Coconut and Flour, stir well. Dip Chicken strips in Egg, then roll in Coconut and Flour mix. Lay strips in a shallow baking dish and drizzle with melted Butter. Bake until golden and chicken is cooked through, about 20-25 minutes. Serve with Apricot Dipping Sauce. Mix 1 cup of Apricot preserves with 2 Tablespoons of Dijon Mustard, blend well.

Smothered Pork Chops & Gravy

Four thick Pork Chops

2 Cups Flour

2 Cups Vegetable Oil

1 teaspoon Sea Salt

1 teaspoon freshly ground Black Pepper

½ cup Water mix with ½ cup Milk

Salt and Pepper Pork Chops and mix about half the Salt and Pepper into Flour. Coat the chops with the Seasoned Flour. In a large frying pan, heat vegetable oil. Fry Pork Chops to brown on both sides and remove from pan. Drain all but about ½ cup of oil from the pan and retain the brown crusts in the frying pan. Return pan to burner and add sufficient seasoned Flour to make a thin roux. When thickened, a cup of half milk and half water to the pan. Reduce heat and add water if mixture becomes too thick. Return Pork Chops to Gravy and cover to finish cooking chops. Serve Smothered Chops over Brown Rice with Gravy.

Brown Rice

Cook and serve in accordance with package directions and based upon number of guests being served.

Fried Okra Salad

1 pound small fresh Okra

2 cups Buttermilk

1 pound Bacon, chopped

1 cup Cornmeal

1 cup Flour

1 ¼ teaspoon Salt, divided

¾ teaspoon Pepper, divided

6 Tomatoes, sliced

1 small coarsely chopped Onion

¼ cup Corn Oil

3 Tablespoons Red Wine Vinegar

3 Tablespoons Honey

1 ½ Tablespoons Dijon Mustard

1 teaspoon Paprika

1 pound Bibb Lettuce

Fresh Basil Sprigs to garnish

Stir together Okra and Buttermilk in a large bowl; let stand for 20 minutes. Drain Okra. Cook chopped Bacon in a large skillet over medium heat until crisp; drain on paper towels. Reserve ¼ cup Bacon drippings. Combine Cornmeal, Flour, 1 teaspoon Salt and ½ teaspoon Pepper in a large zip-top plastic bag; add Okra a few at a time, sealing and shaking to coat each batch.

Pour Oil to a depth of ½ inch into a large, heavy skillet. Fry Okra in batches in hot oil 2 minutes on each side or until golden. Drain well on paper towels.

Process reserved drippings, remaining ¼ teaspoon Salt, remaining ¼ teaspoon Pepper, Onion, Corn Oil, Red Wine Vinegar, Honey, Dijon Mustard in a blender or food processor until smooth, stopping once to scrape down sides. Pour into a 1 cup glass measuring cup. Microwave dressing mixture on high 30 - 45 seconds until thoroughly heated. Line a large serving platter with Lettuce, arrange Tomato and Okra on top. Sprinkle with Bacon and drizzle with warm dressing. Serve immediately.

Coconut Sweet Potato Casserole

2 pounds Sweet Potatoes, cooked, peeled and cut into 1-inch chunks (about 4 cups)

2 Apples, peeled, thin sliced

2/3 cups Maple flavored Pancake and Waffle Syrup

¼ cup Butter, melted

½ teaspoon Salt

2/3 cups Sweetened, Flaked Coconut

Heat oven to 350 degrees. Place Sweet Potatoes in greased 13 X 9 inch baking dish, top with Apples. Mix Syrup, Butter and Salt and pour over Apples. Sprinkle with Coconut, cover. Bake 30 minutes. Uncover, bake 20 – 30 minutes longer or until Apples are tender and Coconut is lightly browned.

Southern Skillet Cornbread

Always make Skillet Cornbread in a Cast Iron Skillet. To prepare skillet preheat in 400 degree oven with 2 Tablespoons shortening and heat until oil begins to smoke or sizzles when a drop of corn meal mixture dropped into the oil.

2 cups Yellow corn Meal

2/3 cup Flour

3 – 4 teaspoons Baking Powder

½ teaspoon Salt

Mix together dry ingredients

Add 2 eggs, beaten

1 1/3 to 1 ½ cup whole milk

1/3 cup Vegetable Oil

Mix together (do not beat) and pour into hot skillet. Bake in 450 degree oven for 10 minutes, then reduce heat to 350 and bake until top crust is brown and cracked and bread is cooked through.

MARKET LIST: Yellow Corn Meal, Whole Milk, Eggs, Vegetable Oil, Flour, Baking Powder, Sweet Potatoes, Coconut, Chicken Breasts, Okra, Tomatoes, Lettuce, Whipping Cream, Pork Chops, Brown Rice, Cinnamon, Tea, Milk, Vanilla, Cocoa, Sugar, Butter, Bananas, Maraschino Cherries, Lemons, Brown Sugar, Baking Powder

Baked Bananas (Plantanos al Horno)

4 firm Bananas

4 Tablespoons Lemon Juice

8 Tablespoons Brown Sugar

½ cup Whipping Cream

8 Maraschino Cherries, chopped

Wash bananas, since they are to be cooked in the peel. Loosen one narrow strip of peeling on each Banana. Carefully take out the Banana, dip in Lemon Juice, roll in Brown Sugar and return to the peel.

Wrap Bananas tightly with aluminum foil and bake in 375 degree oven for ½ our. Remove Bananas from peel, serve in Banana Split dishes topped with Whipped Cream and Cherries.

Fudge Pie

½ cup Sugar

1/3 cup Cocoa

1/3 cup Flour

¼ teaspoon Salt

1 ¼ cup light Corn Syrup

3 Eggs

3 Tablespoons Butter, melted

1 ½ teaspoons Vanilla

½ cup Chopped Pecans and Pecan Halves

(optional)

9 inch Unbaked Pastry Shell

Combine Sugar, Cocoa, Flour, Salt, Syrup, Eggs, Melted Butter and Vanilla in large mixing bowl. Beat briefly just to blend. Add Pecans if desired. Pour into unbaked Pastry Shell. Bake at 350 degrees for about one hour. Arrange Pecan Halves on top of hot pastry if using. Cool.

Hot Cocoa Drink For Large Group

3 cups of Breakfast Cocoa

2 ½ cups Sugar

2 Quarts Boiling Water

10 Quarts of Milk

8 teaspoons Vanilla

Mix Cocoa and Sugar together. Add to the boiling water and boil over low heat stirring occasionally. Add Milk and bring to Scald. Add Vanilla, and beat with egg beater until frothy. Serves group of 30 – 50.

rinted in the United States
y Baker & Taylor Publisher Services